Dedication

For Guylee
may he and many other children benefit from
partnerships that develop for sport and leisure projects in the
years ahead

Developing Partnerships in
Sport and Leisure:
A practical guide

Brigid Simmonds

LONGMAN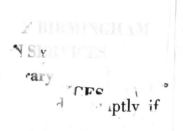

Longman Group Limited
Westgate House, The High,
Harlow, Essex CM20 1YR

Telephone: (0279) 442601
Facsimile: (0279) 444501

First Published 1994

A catalogue record for this book is available from the British Library.

ISBN 0-582-23903-6   18687148

Set in 11/12pt Palatino Roman

Printed by Page Bros, Norwich

Contents

Foreword

The Government believes that the opportunities for imaginative partnership between the public and private sectors, to provide sports and leisure facilities, should be fully exploited. Both in the management of these facilities — to ensure that we have cost effective delivery of quality services — and in the provision of new facilities.

The theme of partnerships will also play a major role in the distribution of Lottery funds. The Sports Council, as the distributing body for sport in England, will be looking to fund capital projects which carry an element of partnership funding.

I am, therefore, pleased to support the theme of this book. I very much hope that some of the examples it provides will encourage local authorities to explore the opportunities that exist for partnerships with the private sector and the valuable financial and managerial input they can provide for new leisure facilities.

Competitive tendering for the management of sports and leisure facilities is an example where it is now increasingly accepted by the public sector that there will be circumstance where the private sector can do a better job than before and, conversely, by the private sector that there are examples where it can learn from the public sector. Initially, there were fears on the one side that local government inevitably kills initiative, and by the other that the profit motive is incompatible with a high quality of service. Both have, of course, been proved wrong.

As the book highlights, the public sector is now seeing examples of private sector companies running CCT contracts for the benefit of the community often providing a degree of investment beyond the scope of the in-house team. This is most encouraging as we approach the second round of CCT.

I believe sport in schools, and extra curricular sport for young people, to be vital in teaching children the values of fair play, good sportsmanship, team-work and team spirit, discipline — particularly self-discipline — and an understanding of the need to abide by the rules. Partnerships such as the Croydon Sports Partnership and in later years the GP Referral Schemes, to which the book refers, can play an essential part in building on these foundations.

This book demonstrates in a number of cases just how valuable partnerships can be in raising the profile of sport and leisure and creating new opportunities for the benefit of the individual and the nation.

Iain Sproat
Parliamentary Under-Secretary of State,
Department of National Heritage

Acknowledgements

I am very grateful to many individuals, in local authorities as members of BISL and in other private sector companies who have given me information to use in this book and who have then checked that what I have written is accurate. Many people have been very frank and open in disclosing information for the case studies, which has been essential if a clear message of good practice is to emerge.

There are a number of people who have given me particular assistance and have read and commented on the entire manuscript. I am very grateful to Dennis Artess, Under Secretary for Economic Development, Leisure and Tourism at the Association of District Councils; to Sally Hart, Head of the Policy Unit at The Sports Council; to Dr Alan Clarke from the Centre for Leisure and Tourism Studies at North London University; to Tony Baden from The Sport and Recreation Division of The Department of National Heritage; to Harm Tegelaars, Managing Director of Archer Leisure; to Adrian Biggs, Partner at Jacques & Lewis (Solicitors) and to Nick Deluca from the Public Affairs Consultancy, Westminster Strategy.

I am as always indebted to John Brackenbury, Chairman of Pubmaster at The Brent Walker Group Plc and Chairman of Business In Sport and Leisure for his continuing support and the time he has put aside to check my manuscript. Finally, I could not have completed this project without the support of my husband Gavin.

1

Introduction

Partnership is a word that reverberates around the offices of nearly all public and private sector organisations and companies in the country. In the dictionary the meaning is shown as sharing, and that has never been easy. The dictionary goes on to an even more difficult definition of 'associations in business where there is a sharing of risks and profit'. Well, since sharing has never been easy, whether it is as a child with a toy or an adult in our personal lives or in business, partnerships are unlikely to be easy either. There are plenty of examples in the private sector of where business partnerships have failed for a variety of reasons. Most of these are associated with the problem of one side wanting more out of the partnership than the other side thought was fair. A successful partnership requires something of a balancing act and each side has to give way if harmony is to be achieved.

If it is difficult to form a partnership in our personal or business lives, when both parties have the same goal, how much more difficult is it to form a partnership when one side is working for a publicly accountable body and the other is a private sector company? One is the custodian of public funds and the other has a remit to make a profit for themselves or their shareholders. And yet, partnerships have been achieved for sport and leisure developments and it is the aim of this book to see how and why they have worked or failed.

This book is, as its title suggests, a practical guide. It is based on the experience of many private sector companies and public sector bodies, who have tried and in many cases succeeded in working together. It is not designed to be an academic tome or to takes sides with either partner. It will look simply at what good practice exists and how both sides have achieved their synergy.

Since Victorian times, local authorities have been the main providers of community sport and leisure facilities in the UK. As a result, the general public expects to have these facilities on their doorstep and to be able to use them at a relatively low cost. For a local community the provision of good, modern sport and leisure facilities is high on their personal agenda, but this provision is not always at the top of their local authorities' political agenda, partly because this provision is discretionary rather than statutory. In the past when local authorities had capital to spend and revenue subsidies to offer as part of large overall budgets, the provision and upkeep of these sport and leisure facilities did not present a problem. For many reasons, however, which we will look at in more detail as this book develops, local authorities are now struggling to cut their budgets. Their priorities must lie with their statutory duty to provide social services, planning control, libraries and refuse collection. They are struggling to maintain existing sport and leisure facilities, let alone build new ones.

Nearly all our Olympic champions and many national teams have learned their skills in swimming pools, sports halls and on outdoor pitches and ice rinks that have been provided and maintained by local authorities. At a time when there is a national clamour for success on the sports field, how can this be reconciled with the lack of funds which are available to provide and maintain these facilities? Can the private sector help? The problem will be enhanced by the requirement, from August 1994, for all children to learn to swim by the age of 11 under the National Curriculum. Do the swimming pools exist in which children can learn to swim and how can we ensure that they are adequately maintained?

The second chapter will look at the history of partnerships in its widest contact. Central Government is keen to encourage partnerships and has set up its own 'Private Sector Finance Initiative'. We will examine Government thinking in this area which covers private sector funding for prisons, roads and the National Health Service. We will look at the role of the Department of National Heritage and the potential for using sport as a basis for economic and inner city regeneration.

So what is the role of the public sector and what is the role of the private sector? Local authorities have to balance a policy of access for everyone with a realistic charge for activities offered. They also have to balance their books and are restricted by Central Government in their spending. The private sector is interested in providing some new facilities, and in some cases operating them. But most private sector companies cannot live with facilities that do not make a profit and unfortunately most sports facilities such as swimming pools, ice rinks and sports halls are very expensive to run.

This book will concentrate on examining possibilities for involving the private sector under three main headings. It will look at planning gain, where a private sector company will agree to provide a sports facility in return for planning permission to build commercial leisure, offices or shops. It will also look at capital receipts, which cover sums of capital received by a local authority in return for the sale of land to the private sector. How can these receipts be used by a local authority to enhance their own sports facilities? There is a strong argument for placing commercial leisure next to local authority sport and leisure facilities and this book will examine the reasons for this and how such partnerships work on the ground. There is a small section of leisure projects which are purely commercial and another short section on partnership schemes which have not worked.

We will examine possibilities for involving the private sector in Compulsory, Competitive Tendering (CCT) contracts. Much has been written on this subject about the lack of private sector partners, the worries of local authorities anxious to keep control over the management of their centres through direct labour organisations and whether standards have really risen when private sector companies do manage facilities. Good management has never been the right of an individual working in the public or private sectors. It is a skill than can be learned, that can mature with more accountability, but there are as many good managers working for local authorities as there are for private sector companies. CCT is, however, a fact of life in the UK and where local authorities are looking for partners in this area, there are examples of good practice. Revenue savings can be achieved by the tendering of contracts and this book will examine examples of this, along with examples of private sector companies prepared to invest capital in local authority owned sports centres, in return for variations or extended contracts.

Lastly, this book will examine other examples of partnership, which can help local authorities decrease annual revenue subsidies required for sport and leisure centres. These range from GP referral schemes, which are becoming increasingly popular and successful, to partnerships with local business for sports development or the promotion of certain events. The *'Health of the Nation'* report sponsored by the Department of Health has highlighted the role sport can play in our daily lives. Local authorities can also benefit from attracting new customers who would perhaps never cross the doors of their leisure centres unless the doctor had not told them that it would be good for their health. What are the revenue implications of this increase in custom?

The introduction of CCT provided a spark for the setting up of **Business In Sport,** a forerunner to the umbrella organisation **Business In Sport and Leisure,** an organisation which represents private sector companies in the leisure industry. It made the private sector operators realise that no-one really understood what type of partnerships they were looking for, or indeed if the private sector had any interest in working with the public sector at all.

This book will examine what exactly the private commercial sport and leisure sector comprises and what type of facilities it does and can operate. It will examine how these facilities can sit side by side and even complement local authority provision. For example, nearly all snooker players learnt their sport in private clubs. Will this be the future for tennis? What is the private sector looking for and how can a local authority attract investment?

A practical book must offer practical advice. A number of chapters will examine how to approach a potential partner from the perspective of a local authority or indeed a private sector company. It will examine the local authority decision making process and how that can affect the speed at which partnerships can proceed. How can the work of an organisation that is the guardian of public funds be matched with a private sector company that often has to satisfy its investors?

An examination of the private sector will look at which commercial leisure facilities will pay the most for land and what the private sector is looking to develop now and in the future. Leisure is and always will be fashionable. For instance, ten pin bowling, which was fashionable in the 1920s, saw a decline in the 1960s and 1970s, saw a boom in the 1980s, but is waning in the 1990s. What does the future hold and how can we predict it?

Although this book will concentrate on partnerships with private sector commercial leisure operators, it will also look at the scope for partnerships with other developers of retail offices and housing. There are also partnerships which work between two public sector bodies, such as local authorities and the NHS, or local authorities and educational establishments. As many different public sector organisations become fund holders in their own right, there is more scope for arrangements to share sports facilities or to join forces to attract funds from private sector companies when there will be a guaranteed rental income.

The use of charitable trusts has many advantages for non-commercial sport facilities, but unfortunately local authorities are prevented by statute from setting them up. By a curious anomaly, there is no problem for a local authority setting up a charitable trust for an arts centre, but opinion voiced by the Audit Commission is that this ability to set up trusts for the arts cannot be extended to sport. A chapter of this book will examine how this works and the value of trusts where commercial and non-commercial leisure sit side by side.

There is no doubt that the benefits of partnership can be immense and satisfy each partner. This book will look at the benefits, the strategic role of the local authority, acting as an enabler and taking advantage over its control of planning permission. It will offer guidelines on how to set up and develop partnerships both for the local authority and the private sector company. There will always be potential problems and a chapter will examine what these are and how they can be overcome. What are the sensitivities and how do you do decide what is sacrosanct?

Perhaps most importantly, there will be a number of case studies. These are not meant to be case studies of procedures, but more in-depth analysis about how each partner approached their particular project, how they learned to work together and the benefits at the end of the day. A breadth of vision is required to make partnerships work or even to think that opportunities exist. In researching this book, it has become apparent that there are many more public and private sector companies and organisations that are looking at partnerships than anyone can have imagined. Whatever their political colour, many local authorities are embracing the idea of partnership as a way forward in the future. As the economy moves out of recession, the private sector is looking for development opportunities. Sport and leisure has the potential to be an enabler in development, if these opportunities are grasped. This book does not pretend to have all the answers, but it aims to offer up ideas worth further consideration, as we approach the millennium.

2

The history of partnership – the wider context

Post Second World War, the United Kingdom has been dominated by social provision which can provide assistance where necessary, from cradle until the grave. The introduction of the National Health Service, social security payment for sickness and maternity leave, the state pension and unemployment benefit have all been paid for through taxation, both direct and indirect and these benefits have been seen as a cushion on which we can all lay our heads in time of need. On a local basis, these national policies have been extended to everything from free milk at school to grants for home improvements and even facilities in which we spend our leisure hours.

This deliberately black and white picture, without mention of the various shades of grey, is designed to put into context the provision of sport and leisure facilities by local authorities. With such a steer from Central Government, it was both right and proper that not only our working lives were looked after, but also our leisure hours.

Whatever our political persuasion, much has changed since Margaret Thatcher came to power in the early 1980s. Gradually the idea that the state takes care of us from cradle until grave has been eroded for various reasons, which are either right or wrong depending on your political point of view. Demographics have had something to do with the change. Between 1989 and 1997 the population of the United Kingdom is predicted to increase by 1.2 million to 58.4 million, a two per cent growth. Looking at these population figures in more detail, there will be an increase in the number of children under the age of 15, but a decrease in the number of 15-19 years olds and 20-29 year olds. As we approach the end of the century, we face the prospect of an increased number of 'golden oldies' — those over the age of retirement. The Government has argued that these changes mean that those in work will have an increased burden to pay for an increasing majority, many of whom will be either out of work, too young to work, sick or retired. There are, however, some academic institutes who dispute the effects of these changes on the welfare state.

This change in demographics has been accompanied by the effects of the recession which began in the late 1980s. Together, these factors have led to a complete reappraisal of what services the state should provide for free and how these services can be maintained over the next decade. Faced by a perceived public sector borrowing requirement of over £50 billion, (this figure has now decreased and accountancy rules for its calculation may change in the future), the Government has been forced to look at ways of reducing their own budgets and those of the public sector organisations that they control. They have also been forced to look at how best they can harness financial support from private sector companies and persuade them to invest in facilities traditionally provided by the public sector.

The 50% rule

For sport and leisure, the first tinkering with traditional thinking came with the introduction of the **1989 Local Government and Housing Act,** which effected how local authorities could spend the capital receipts they received from the private sector. Local authorities have always been land owners and the sale of this land either for capital or for a receipt in kind, more commonly known as planning gain, has helped fund their own capital programme.

In 1989, Central Government, concerned at the rise in local authority debt, which they saw as a major contributor to the Public Sector Borrowing Requirement deficit, decided to curb how much of the capital receipt a local authority could spend on its own projects. The **1989 Local Government and Housing Act,** which came into force in 1990, introduced the so-called 50% rule. In other words, local authorities could only spend 50 per cent of the capital they received from the sale of land for all projects except housing, where they could only use 25 per cent. The 1989 Act also banned the use of lease-back and barter agreements, which had been commonly used for sport and leisure projects in the 1980s. The effect of this rule was two-fold. Firstly, local authorities became loathe to sell land to the private sector if they could only use part of the proceeds. Secondly, as land prices fell with the recession there was even less reason to sell land at all. The private sector has always maintained that the fall in land prices was inevitable and that in any case, leisure cannot afford the land prices achieved by other developments such as retail or office accommodation. Land prices for leisure are now at more realistic levels. Both views have fuelled the uneasy relationship between the private sector and the public sector and at least one local authority has spoken of the desire of private sector companies to force them into a 'fire sale' of land to solve their budgetary problems. There is obviously a middle path to be found by both sides.

In an effort to ride the recession, the 50% rule was relaxed by the Chancellor of the Exchequer in his Autumn Statement of 1992. The relaxation was made specifically to assist the construction industry and the Government estimated that it would stimulate extra capital spending by local authorities of over £1.75 billion over the next three and a half years. The relaxation only affected capital receipts gained from the day after the Autumn Statement, until 31st December 1993. It was not retrospective.

Business In Sport and Leisure, with backing from The Sports Council, The CBI and others, led the campaign to have this relaxation introduced, as it believed that the 50% rule created a real barrier for commercial leisure companies looking to buy land from local authorities. As this book progresses, it will become apparent that many private sector leisure companies consider that local authorities own most of the best sites for private sector sport and leisure development. The 50% rule was therefore perceived as setting up a real barrier for leisure companies looking for new development sites.

Many felt that the relaxation was not for long enough. The notes from DoE accompanying the relaxation stated that local authorities had to receive the capital before 31st December 1993, or in the case of a notional receipt, have signed a deal. In other words, if a local authority sold a piece of land to a private sector developer for ten-pin bowling, it had to receive the capital before 31st December. If on the other hand the local authority asked the private sector operator to build a children's play ground in return for the land, then the deal must have been signed, but the children's play ground need not have been built.

Anyone connected with local authority decision making will realise how short a year is in their cycle. To stimulate new projects, rather than to take advantage of planned partnerships arrangements, within the year is very difficult. It took many local authorities six months to understand what this rule meant for them and certainly what it could mean in terms of leisure provision rather than for housing projects. Once they had decided to seek interest from the private sector for a development site, or even if they were approached direct by a private sector company, they then had to advertise the site to other operators in order to achieve the best price. Within a local authority certain powers may be delegated to officers to make certain decisions, but it is inevitable that several committees will have to agree to sell land, for what price and for what purpose. By the time the legal agreement has been reached it is unlikely that the process will have taken much less than a year.

Throughout 1993, many organisations and individuals continued to press the Government to extend the relaxation into 1994 on the grounds that the construction industry was still in recession and that the target of £1.75 billion over the next three and half years was unlikely to be realised. In a written House of Commons answer, the DoE stated that around £1.3 billion of usable receipts were obtained during the period 13 November 1992 to 31 July 1993, of which about £0.7 billion represented additional spending power as a result of the relaxation. This information also suggests that local authorities currently expect to obtain around £2.3 billion of usable receipts during the whole period of the relaxation (13 November 1992 to 31 December 1993), of which about £1.3 billion represents extra spending power arising from the relaxation. It will always be difficult to estimate how many of these projects really were new, i.e. conceived after the relaxation was announced or indeed how many of the projects funded were sport and leisure based. As we will see in later chapters some partnerships for leisure have taken between five and fifteen years to come to fruition.

It became clear, however, that the Government had no intention of extending the relaxation into 1994.

Compulsory Competitive Tendering (CCT)

The second politically endangered change which has affected the provision of sport and leisure has been the introduction of Compulsory Competitive Tendering(CCT) for sport and leisure facilities. It was in 1987 that the Government were thinking of introducing CCT for local authority owned sport and leisure centres and expected great interest from the private sector. There were two main problems with these expectations. The first was the degree of expertise required by companies entering into this market. As we will see later on in this book, when we consider partnerships offered by CCT contractors, the majority of companies in this field are either small companies who only operate one or two contracts, or they are major companies who specialise in management contracts. Many of these larger companies, such as SERCO, have past experience and expertise in operating other contracts such as grounds maintenance or refuse collection to draw on when they moved into CCT contracts for sport and leisure. For the majority of major leisure operating companies no expertise existed in the late 1980s to take on these short contracts and most of these companies own what they operate and ownership was not offered as part of the deal.

The second problem is that the level of subsidy required to run local authority sport and leisure centres on the traditional basis of providing something that the whole community can use no-matter what their means requires considerable subsidy. Most local authority-run swimming pools require an annual operating subsidy of between £150,000-350,000. As local authority budgets have become tighter, so the annual operating subsidy has come under the spot light. However, it is easier for a local authority to deal with this on-going deficit than for a private sector company, who often has investors to satisfy. Private sector companies must make profits and although many will become involved in partnership arrangements and provide capital to build a new sports centre, few can live with an ongoing operating deficit. Ideologically, there will always be a problem with establishing partnerships, when on one hand the local authority is committed to providing sport and leisure as a service which everyone, of whatever financial means, can use and on the other hand accepting that in order for everyone to use it, prices must be low. This not only provides a problem for any competing private sector facilities, but it is inevitable that pricing will remain low and therefore a subsidy will always be required. Perhaps the future lies in extended use of 'Passport to Leisure' schemes which allow free access to those who really need it. Prices for other people using the centre could be increased.

The Private Sector Finance Initiative

The introduction of CCT in 1990 was designed by the Government to open the door to a philosophy of local authorities acting as enablers, rather than just as providers. This idea has been further extended and broadened by the introduction of the 'Private Sector Finance Initiative'[1] as one answer to attracting private sector investment. On the whole, this initiative is aimed at major projects in the transport, the construction industry and the NHS. Examples given by the Treasury of how this initiative promotes development, include the £23 million

Skye bridge which will be run as a toll bridge and the proposed £400 million second Forth road bridge.[2] These initiatives do break new ground in the way that they encourage financially free-standing projects, which in the past could only have been provided by the public sector and for which the private sector was unable to bid. The reason why these projects were always publicly funded was that there had to be a comparison between the cost of funding the project by the public sector before a private sector bid could be considered. Because, inevitably, the Government and other public sector organisations could always borrow more cheaply through gilts and bonds, the comparison went in favour of public funding. The private Sector Finance Initiative alters this view.

It also overtly encourages joint ventures where the control of the project rests with the private sector and where the Government's contribution could be equity, the transfer of existing assets or a combination of both. This allows public sector organisations such as the NHS to buy a complete service from the private sector, for example the setting up of kidney dialysis equipment, leased from a private sector company, rather than the hospital having to buy the equipment itself. Services such as laundry, catering, sterile supplies, waste incineration and contract energy management are to be offered to private sector competition. There is no longer a requirement to compare against a public sector comparator for these services. Until April 1993, every project involving capital spending over £250,000 required central approval from the NHS Management Executive, but now private finance schemes with a capital value of up to £10 million can be approved by Regional Health Authorities and outposts of the central NHS Management Executive. This encourages joint ventures where residences are sub-let to staff, excess car parks sold to private companies and the provision of what, in the past, have been services provided only by the public sector such as design, construction and management of new prisons or accommodation of day-to-day care for the elderly.

Once the relevant Government papers which explain all these issues have been understood, there is a slight feeling that sport and leisure has been treading this path for some years and perhaps has something to teach other sections of industry. It will become clear as this book progresses how close a co-operation has and does exist. However, in developing the theme, the Government also sees the Private Finance Initiative as a way in which it can identify schemes which it wishes to promote and feels are ripe for private sector investment. Some of these schemes are promoted by the Treasury, but other Government Departments are invited to encourage bids for their own individual schemes. For the sport and leisure industry the most interesting of these ideas have come from the Department of the Environment, who are looking at a variety of mixed-use developments throughout the UK. For example, Bristol Harbourside is a regeneration project where the City Council and other private sector companies are looking for a scheme which will create employment, housing and leisure in a quality environment. The London Borough of Lewisham is looking for a redevelopment of the Lewisham Odeon site for a mix of shopping, office and leisure facilities.

The Private Finance Initiative does not provide for a new source of funding, but it does identify projects where some assistance may be given by, for example, an Urban Development Corporation who might finance land acquisition, land reclamation and services for road access. The renovation of a listed building can be eligible for a City Grant[3] and perhaps a repair grant from English Heritage.[4]

So far, the Department of National Heritage has not suggested any schemes for funding under this initiative and that is probably because they are not fund holders and therefore are unable to 'pump prime' potential joint developments for the private sector. It may be, however, that the Sports Council identifies specific sites suitable for joint ventures or for private sector investment as part of their plans to identify new developments to be part funded from the National Lottery, although it is difficult to see how this can work when the guidelines for the distribution of funds from the Lottery require all applicants to be unsolicited. The private sector leisure industry is more likely to respond to a project which will go ahead within the next year than it is to a project that requires major infrastructure and will not go ahead within the next ten years. When Manchester was bidding for the 2000

Olympic Games, their partners in the Olympic projects were mainly from the construction and development industries. The anticipation was that specific leisure projects would be developed in conjunction with the leisure industry as the year 2000 approached and individual opportunities could be identified.

The Department of National Heritage

The creation of the Department of National Heritage following the General Election in 1992 has been a significant step in the history of partnership and the role of central Government in this sphere. A series of sports ministers, based in the Department of the Environment and then the Department of Education with very little power, no budget and other ministerial responsibilities, has not served the sport and leisure industry well. The formation of a new department under a Cabinet Minister whose responsibilities embraced sport, leisure, tourism, heritage and the arts was very much welcomed throughout the industry. Although the new Department of National Heritage only has a limited budget (other than for funding grant-aid bodies under its control), it is trying hard to bring together the interests of the wider leisure industry and as such ensure greater co-operation between them. For the private sector, many companies own interests which cover sport, leisure, tourism, the arts and heritage and it has always seemed sensible for these industries to be dealt with by one department. In the future the DNH will also be responsible for the policy and success of the Lottery, for its regulation through the Office of the National Lottery (OFLOT) and for the distribution of funds through the five nominated bodies.

Although sport and leisure has never been at the top of the political agenda, there is beginning to be a greater realisation of its role across all walks of life. This is in no little way helped by John Major as a Prime Minister who is himself keen on sport and who therefore has been prepared to encourage sporting themes. The sport and leisure industry has a job to do to promote its relevance across a wider spectrum of life. Partnership projects which not only provide for those interested in sport, but also encourage the health of the nation, and the use of sport in attacking the causes of the breakdown in law and order facing this country which generally impinge on every walk of life must be encouraged, if sport is to aspire to greater political interests from other departments of state.

Sport and urban regeneration

In the 1980s, the Garden Festivals, which can only come under the heading of leisure and tourism, were used as a centre piece for urban regeneration. Festivals in Liverpool, Stoke on Trent, Gateshead, Glasgow and Ebbw Vale were enormously successful and formed a basis for regeneration that could not have been created by any other activity or type of development. In the case of Stoke on Trent, this led to the development of a business park by St Modwen Developments, with commercial leisure operated by The Rank Organisation and First Leisure Corporation, including multiplex cinema, ten-pin bowling, amusements and a variety of restaurants. Rank Leisure also own and operate a waterworld (leisure swimming pool) for the local community.

Ebbw Vale was the last Garden Festival, because it was considered that the large sums of public money required to set up Garden Festivals did not justify the end result, even if, as was the case in Ebbw Vale, it would be difficult to see how such regeneration could have been achieved without leisure and tourism use.

In a recent paper, James Froomberg, a Partner at KPMG Peat Marwick, noted the high cost of using sport and leisure as a **driver** of regeneration in inner cities [5]. One of the best known speciality shopping and leisure developments in the world was in Baltimore, developed by the Rouse Corporation in the 1980s. However, this project required $60 million of public sector money at 1980 prices for some of the major leisure projects (museum, aquarium and conference centre) which anchored the development. In the UK, Sheffield used sport and leisure as a driver for urban regeneration when it staged the World Student Games and built the Ponds Forge Pool, an arena and the Don Valley Stadium, but the cost to the public purse was around £140 million.

It is understandable why central and local government shy away from massive projects which will require large amounts of public sector money without extensive economic and design master planning. There has to be a substantial justification of the use of public funds to ensure that, over time, the private investment and all the other facets of urban regeneration follow.

This view must be balanced, however, by the substantial regeneration which such projects can bring. In Manchester, KPMG showed that by the time the 2000 Olympics were staged some £4 billion would be invested, 80 per cent by the private sector, creating 108,600 person-years of employment. Even when the bid was unsuccessful, a total expenditure of £200 million was achieved in the region of a ratio of nearly 3:1 private to public sector expenditure. All these projects obviously also have unmeasurable benefits which are difficult to define, such as after-use of the venues by the local community, increased tourism, the potential for attracting inward investment, the legacy of IT and media facilities and the volunteer workforce and in-kind contributions.

It is interesting that more recently sport and leisure development has formed a central theme in bids for City Challenge money. In researching his paper, James Froomberg analysed the 20 winning authorities who sought a total of £67 million for sport and leisure projects from Government spread over five years. On average, the 20 winners therefore estimated that 9 per cent of their £37.5 million funds would be used specifically for sport, leisure and related projects. Only one of the twenty winners had no specific intention of using any of their investment for sport and leisure. As well as the Government's £67 million, the successful authorities estimate that these specific leisure projects will attract non-Government leisure investment of around £126 million — or roughly a 2:1 ratio of private sector to public sector investment.

When asked, the Department of the Environment denied that the part played by sport and leisure had any bearing on their decision to chose the winning bids. There is no doubt, however, that subconsciously sport and leisure is considered a strong **component** element of inner city regeneration, albeit on a smaller scale to what has been attempted in Manchester or Sheffield. It is seen as a useful component, however, rather than a driver. It should also be noted that the unsuccessful City Challenge bidders still included 8.3 per cent of their total bidding for sport and leisure projects. Unlike the winners, however, they expected a private-public sector ratio of investment in the leisure projects of 9:1, rather than 2:1. It may be that the City Challenge losers had unrealistic expectations of the level of private sector leisure investment which could be levered.

The sport and leisure industry needs to promote the value of sport and leisure in inner city regeneration as a component and, as we shall see in chapter 6, there are some good examples of where such regeneration has been achieved with partnership schemes.

Summary

If we are to summarise the wider and political importance of partnerships in the UK, we must reach several conclusions:

● The political climate has changed, probably irrevocably, from the time when sport and leisure provision was solely in the hands of local government to a time when Central Government is looking towards the private sector for investment.

● The Government has tried to encourage private sector investment in sport and leisure through the introduction of CCT and other initiatives such as the Private Sector Finance Initiative, although the imposition of the 50% rule is seen as a disincentive for local authorities to sell their land to private sector companies

- The setting up of the Department of National Heritage has been a boon to sport, leisure, the arts, heritage and tourism. There is more work to be done to highlight the important part sport and leisure can play in all walks of life and how it can impinge on the work of other Government Departments.

- Above all, partnerships in sport and leisure are rather better developed than many others which the Government is now keen to establish under the Private Sector Finance Initiative. Much has been achieved to establish a firm platform for the future.

Notes and references

1. The Private Sector Finance Initiative — Private Finance Unit, HM Treasury — 071 270 4779/270 5531/270 5527

2. The Department of the Environment Private Finance Unit, Room A707, 7th Floor, Romney House, 43 Marsham Street, London SW1P 3PY

3. City Grants — administered by English Partnerships — 16/18 Old Queen Street, London SW1H 9HP — 071 976 7070

4. English Heritage — Fortress House, 23 Savile Row, London W1X 1AB — 071 973 3000. Grants from English Heritage are administered on a regional basis.

5. *'Urban Regeneration through Sport and Leisure'* by James Froomberg, Partner KPMG Peat Marwick, available from BISL, 7 Soho Street, London W1V 5FA

3

Provision of sport in the UK

Since Victorian times, the provision of sport and leisure facilities in the UK has been in the hands of local authorities. The Sports Council estimates that local authorities provide the vast majority of the estimated 3,000 indoor premises and innumerable outdoor areas for sport in the UK.[1]

Sport is, however, not a statutory provision for local authorities in England and Wales, although its provision is statutory in Scotland. In other words, it is a fact that local authorities have to provide certain services such as refuse collection, education and social services to certain standards set down by central Government. They do not, however, have to provide sports facilities. These services are considered discretionary and it is left up to the local authority to decide what its provision will be. The Association of District Councils has been arguing for some time that sport and all other leisure services should be a statutory provision throughout the UK. The answer from Central Government has been that they are not sure that standards of provision in Scotland are any higher than they are in England and Wales and that minimum standards would not be of any great assistance.

The range of provision varies enormously throughout the UK and, of course, local authorities are assisted in the decision making about provision by the Sports Council, both centrally and through the regional offices of the Sports Council.

Until the mid 1970s, local authorities concentrated on building facilities which were, in the main, designed purely for sport and fitness (sports halls, swimming pools, ice rinks) leisure was not a word used at all. Most 'leisure' facilities (health suites, sauna worlds, cinemas, ten-pin bowling, bingo, nightclubs) were built and operated by private sector companies. This began to change in the mid 1970s, when the first leisure swimming pools were built in this country which were designed for fun, rather than for pure sport and fitness. The Sun Centre at Rhyl was designed to match a market where there was a small indigenous population of some 75,000, but 4.2 million visitors during the summer months. A huge leisure pool, with café, flumes and a monorail which runs right round inside the building, the Sun Centre did until last year cover its operating costs and had around 400,000 visitors, opening at Easter and closing at the end of October. The centre cost £6 million at 1980 prices and was paid for within eight years The leisure provision has proved to be a focus for the regeneration of Rhyl, which is now half way through a seven year £23 million investment plan.

The Sun Centre at Rhyl is a good example of how the private sector first became involved in local authority provision through a new wave of architecture. Gillinson Barnet, based in Leeds, designed and built several new leisure pools around this time, where not only was the type of facility important, but so was the market it served. Another example was the Crowtree centre at Sunderland, which has not only a leisure pool, but also an ice rink, sports halls, squash court, flat green bowling, climbing wall and cafe. It still takes more than 2 million visitors each year, which is more than any other local authority-owned sports centre in the country.

Out of Gillinson Barnet came several architectural practices which contributed much to the design of local authority sport and leisure centres in the 1980s. Sargent and Potiriadis,

11

Graham and Lambert, Miller Associates and Charles Smith, along with the Newcastle based partnership Faulkner Browns, took over much of the work of local authority in-house architects. Local authorities realised that designing for sport and leisure was a specialised business, not always suited to their in-house team. As time has gone by, many local authorities have contracted-out all their architectural services.

In the late 1970s and 1980s local authorities did their best to build new and modern sport and leisure facilities for their local communities. Although not a statutory duty, the provision of good modern facilities is definitely a political vote-winner. A Sports Council survey revealed that in 1989/90 local authority capital spending on all services (at today's prices) was over £5 billion and of that over £350 million was spent on sport and leisure facilities. By 1992/93, capital spending for all services was down to £2.5 billion whilst capital spending for sport and leisure projects had declined to under £100 million.

Obviously tighter control from Central Government, highlighted in the previous chapter, along with the recession, has been partly responsible for this decline. It should be noted that few if any of the large sport and leisure centres built in the late 1970s or early 1980s were provided with any sort of funding from the private sector. They were funded purely by local authorities and their upkeep paid for out of revenue budgets. The Sports Council survey, which also considered revenue expenditure, showed that there was very little decline between the 1989/90 levels of expenditure and 1992/93. A similar survey this year is likely to show that revenue expenditure is now falling and when it is considered that The Amateur Swimming Association estimate that existing swimming pools will require about £1,200 to £1,300 million reinvestment at 1992 prices during the next decade simply to keep them in a safe and usable condition, one wonders where these funds will come from.

The Department of National Heritage and the Government as a whole would dispute the figures put forward by the Sports Council and believe that the picture is not nearly as black as it is painted. Their view would be that local authority funding for sport has declined, but that this is due purely to local authorities concentrating on other priorities. The aim of this book is not to act as an apology for either camp. Irrespective of whether you believe that local authorities should only act as enablers of sports facilities and therefore it is right that their funding of these projects has declined or that we are facing a dark hole where our sport and leisure provision is in an irrevocable state of decline, the fact remains that local authority funding for sport and leisure facilities is falling and this opens up an avenue for attracting investment from the private sector.

At the end of the 1980s, local authorities began to look more seriously at what assistance could be attracted from the private sector, mainly in the form of land deals. The figures for capital spending in 1989/90 are most definitely distorted by the effect of the expected *1989 Local Government and Housing Act*, which came into force in April 1990 and many local authorities took advantage of land deals prior to the enforcement of this act. Local authorities began to look more seriously at leisure as well as sports provision and many of the new centres were built with facilities for both. Statistics show that most leisure pools are used by 60 per cent children and 40 per cent adults, while the statistics are reversed in competition swimming pools. Local authorities began to see the value of building sport and leisure centres which would cost them less to run and so included facilities such as modern cafe/bars, health suites, fitness clubs and sauna worlds which had been so successful for the private market in the 1980s. The growth in understanding of the needs of defined market groups such as mothers and small children and 'Golden Oldies', or those taking early retirement, for whom relaxing facilities like saunas and steam rooms were much more attractive, added something to these trends.

It is worth at this stage describing a centre which was built in the late 1980s with funding from the private sector provided as part of a land deal, producing a capital receipt for the local authority.

The Coral Reef, Bracknell

Bracknell Forest Borough Council owned a housing site close to the town centre which they considered too valuable for council housing. The tenants were re-housed in more modern accommodation and the Council held a development competition for the re-development of the site. Peel Developments won and designed a non-food retail warehouse scheme, with a superstore and commercial leisure (ten-pin bowling, 10 screen multiplex cinema, restaurant, fast food unit and disco). The commercial leisure centre is called The Point and operated by Bass Leisure. At 1989 prices, this deal raised approximately £6 million which was allocated to a new leisure pool.

The Council had adequate facilities for competition swimming and teaching and so held a competition for the design of a new leisure pool, widely regarded as a 'state of the art' centre, 'The Coral Reef'. The centre was designed by Sargent & Potiriadis. In its first year it achieved well above its target and had 570,000 visitors, so that it easily covered its operating costs.

There are two lessons which should be learned from this project which will re-occur time and time again as this book progresses. The first is that Bracknell Forest Borough Council were determined to provide 'state of the art' leisure facilities for their community. They were obviously in a fortunate position, having good road and rail links (the M4 and M3 both lead easily to Bracknell). Bracknell was also, in the 1980s, in a boom area, part of the 'golden triangle' in the South East of England and as such attracted much interest from private sector property developers, which in turn produced capital receipts. In retrospect, there is no doubt that the success of Bracknell in subsequent years to attract industry and people to live in the area has been in part due to the excellent sport and leisure facilities that the town has. The Council also attracted private sector leisure provision from the John Nike Centre which is an international standard ice rink and dry ski centre and from ISL Leisure, who built The Royal County of Berkshire Health and Racquets Clubs, opposite Coral Reef.

Secondly, the Coral Reef leisure pool came about through the determination of the leisure committee, and Councillor Alan Ward who was until recently Chairman of the Association of District Council's Leisure Committee and from the late Director of Leisure Mike Evans. For any leisure building which requires assistance from the private sector, there have to be one or two people within the Council who are totally committed to seeing the scheme completed and act as leaders for the project.

New types of sport and leisure facilities

Whoever pays for it, The Coral Reef was a land mark in the changing type of provision. Whether it be through refurbishment or new build, local authorities began to look at leisure as well as sport provision and consider who used their centres and why. In many ways the local authority leisure officer came of age. In the past, the provision of sports facilities was all about excellence. Children needed sport facilities so that they could be taught how to swim, play games, take part in athletics and many other sports. Excellence was all about producing Olympic champions and members of international teams. There was less emphasis on participation, although evidence existed that centres such as Crowtree, which provided sports facilities which could be used by all members of the family, were a great success. Children could swim, or ice skate, parents could join them, play badminton or have a more sedentary game of bowls.

This trend towards local authority provision for leisure, as well as sport, is one that is very important and should not be dismissed. Too many people see leisure as something that is frivolous which should not be confused with sport, when in fact it can contribute as much to adolescence and adult life as pure sport, particularly if you have no natural interest in or aptitude for sport. How many children learn to swim, but are then bored by swimming up and down in a conventional pool? Their future lies in an annual dip in the English Channel in August. Leisure swimming pools offer so much more fun, and yet they are still offering exercise. This is not to say in any way that our competitive sports facilities are any less important, but leisure sport facilities have their part to play. They are just as likely to keep children off the streets, keep them active and contribute to making active pursuits part of a healthy adult life. Leisure pools also offer a much 'softer' introduction to water for the very young and even the very old, who never learn to swim, by having a beach entry to the pool and very shallow (and non-intimidating water). Even learner pools seem deep to a four year-old.

In citing Crowtree as a centre which provides facilities for all ages and interests, there is a growing trend, where possible, to construct sport and leisure facilities side by side on the same site. This is often referred to as 'critical mass' and Crowtree is a very good example of this. In Crowtree, all the facilities are in one building operated by the local authority. In the 1990s, there are more opportunities for the development of privately operated leisure facilities to be located adjacent to local authority owned sports facilities. In chapter 6, one of the case studies considered is the Colchester Leisure World. At Colchester, we will see a site which has sports hall, multi-purpose hall (also suitable for the arts), leisure and conventional swimming and sauna world, all provided by the local authority. They sit side by side on the same site as ten-pin bowling and a McDonalds restaurant, which have been built and are operated by the private sector. The attraction is that there is more to offer all members of a family or group and indeed that there is so much on offer that visitors will return. As we all know, repeat visits are a very important component of successful sport or leisure provision.

Strategic thinking and planning for sport and leisure

When the Department of the Environment published their draft Planning Policy Guidance Note (PPG) number 17 on Sport and Recreation in 1991, BISL commented on the important role to be played by local authorities in strategic planning for sport and leisure facilities. Planning Approval is the master card held by all local authorities and a key element of partnerships for sport and leisure. It is an obvious reason why the private sector must contact a local authority for approval for whatever it is trying to build.

In the past there seemed little connection between the ideas of the local authority leisure departments for the development of sport and the role of the planning department. Planners were often involved in either producing development plans for a particular site, which might include commercial leisure, or in granting planning permission for a private sector company for a commercial leisure operation which was situated on land which the local authority owned or which was bought from a private sector owner. Too often there was little discussion between the planner and the leisure officer. Yet there was and is much to be gained from making this connection.

A local authority leisure department can often see potential for attracting private sector investment, through the positioning of commercial leisure next to a local authority owned sports centre (like at Colchester, in which one helps to fund the other). It is no good then going to the planning department and finding that they have given planning permission for ten-pin bowling and a McDonalds elsewhere in the area, or that they have invited a developer to put together a proposal for a mixed-use development, which contains commercial leisure.

The importance of planners working with their leisure departments has become even more important since the introduction of Unitary Development Plans, Local Development Plans and Structure Development Plans. In the past, if a private sector operator had planning permission refused, it could have appealed and often won the appeal, even if the local authority contended that the land was unsuitable for leisure. Under the new system, if the site is not zoned for leisure use in the local plan, then it is far more likely to be determined in accordance with the local plan and planning permission to be refused. This is a two edged sword. It gives local authorities greater powers to dismiss unwanted interest in a particular site or area, but it also means that unless it includes leisure in its plans then it will find it difficult to attract private sector investors within its boundaries.

Local authority leisure departments have a crucial role to play as enablers. Not only are they in a position to assess what sports provision is required and whether there is any advantage to be gained from potential private sector investment in commercial leisure. They are also in a position to assess the leisure potential of their council, looking not only at sports provision, but also at the possible gaps in private sector leisure provision, to see if they can attract operators to fill these gaps and offer something in return, either as a capital receipt, or as a planning gain. It is important to remember that many commercial leisure operators believe that some of the best sites for leisure are owned by local authorities. It is up to the local authority to take advantage of this. At the end of the day, if the leisure department is the department that attracts the private sector investment then it has a much stronger case for ensuring that part of the capital receipt achieved is ploughed back into its own sports provision.

Unitary authorities

The introduction of unitary authorities will have a major effect on local authority provision for sport and leisure. Up until now, the main providers of community leisure have been district and metropolitan authorities, with county councils mainly involved in the provision of school sports facilities. The local management of schools has created its own problems for both sets of authorities and the Sports Council. As schools took control of their own budgets, adjacent sports centres went with it and suddenly the 'dual use' centre, which was perhaps part funded by a grant from the Sports Council and received revenue support from the local authority, disappeared. This caused particular problems for centres built between 1986 and 1989. These anomalies have been largely taken care of through the new Education Act which protects school sports facilities where the property was part owned by the local authority and the school. Some difficulties can still occur if the school owns the property and just has an agreement for dual use by the community, and perhaps this is a situation where an improved relationship will be created by a unitary authority. There are additional problems where schools opt out under GMS (Grant-Maintained Schools)

New unitary authorities should bring together many of the services which will be a reflection of the departmental concerns of the Department of National Heritage. One authority would be responsible for education, youth, sport, leisure and planning and the experience of metropolitan authorities suggests that this can and will work well. Considerable concern has been expressed by many organisations that the expertise that presently exists in district leisure departments should not swallowed up by a desire to reduce direct costs through amalgamating various services and departments. In 25 out of the 36 metropolitan authorities, leisure services are separate from education departments and many existing district authorities believe that this should remain the case in the new unitary authorities. In some districts, it is already recognised that there could be great value in bringing in community education and youth services into the leisure services group. It has always seemed rather impractical that an organisation such as the Duke of Edinburgh Award Scheme deals with youth services and has so few dealings with local authority leisure departments, when at least two elements of the award, the expedition and the physical recreation, are so closely related to their work. However, for many local authorities and elected members in Metropolitan Districts, it is clear that Leisure Services are incompatible with Education and there would be no benefit in joining the two services.

When the Audit Commission produced their diagram showing the 'Local Authority Support for Sport', they saw the local authority sport and leisure departments as acting as enablers for the voluntary and private sectors. They are shown as unlocking existing school facilities and bringing them into public use, bringing existing buildings such as church halls and community halls into use for sport, upgrading their own facilities and co-operating with other authorities. For the voluntary sector they provide grants, loans and peppercorn rents and they can liaise with the private sector, considering sports facilities as part of larger developments on land provided by the local authority. There is a real concern that these services will be lost if the expertise of existing local authority sport and leisure departments disappears.

It is a sad reflection that sport fails to reach the top of the political agenda. The services of sport and leisure departments hardly receive a mention when new structures for unitary authorities are discussed. This is a problem that needs addressing. In a relatively short time, existing leisure services teams have achieved very high professional standards which should not be lost.

Additional sources of funding for sport

A history of partnership for sport would not be complete without some consideration of funding available from other bodies offering grant aid, funding from the European Community and other public sector bodies.

At the 1993 Institute of Baths and Recreation Management Conference in Scarborough (IBRM, now renamed ISRM — the Institute of Sport and Recreation Management[2], Cyril Villiers, Regional Director of the Yorkshire and Humberside Region of the Sports Council gave an excellent twenty minute presentation under the title of 'Finding Funding'.

Some grants are still available from the EC and the Sports Council publication 'Brussels in Focus: EC Access for Sport'[3] published in December 1992 can advise applicants where to look. The European Regional Development Fund assists with projects in areas suffering from under-development or industrial decline — RECHAR (running down of coal industry areas) and RENEVAL (former ship building areas). There are various grants available to assist with Youth in Europe, like the Petra Action 1 scheme which offers vocational training placements for three weeks in another European country between school and work. The European Social Fund offers assistance to people with disabilities through HORIZON, for women through NOW and for training in new occupations and skills through EUROFORM. Details of all these schemes and, where necessary, contacts for further assistance can be obtained from Regional Offices of The Sports Council.

In the UK, as already mentioned, City Challenge has provided funding for sport, as has the Urban programme, Urban Partnership, the Derelict Land Grant, Contaminated Land Grant etc. A new body, English Partnerships[4] launched in November 1993, will promote the development of vacant, derelict and contaminated land throughout England and bring land and buildings back into productive use, stimulate local enterprise, create job opportunities and improve the environment. English Partnerships will take over City Grant which was previously operated by DoE and in due course will take over the Derelict Land Grant and English Estates. It is slightly confusing that this body, to be headed up by Lord Walker, was originally set up as the Urban Regeneration Agency.

At the end of 1993, the Government also announced new regional offices which will be set up from April 1994. Each of the new ten regions will have a sponsor minister and a new Single Regeneration Budget will ensure that many of the grants previously offered by different Government Departments will be available from a regional office. Twenty different programmes will be amalgamated to be administered by the new regional offices.

Looking more specifically at funds available for Sport, funds can be made available from the Football Trust[5], the Lawn Tennis Foundation[6], the Lord Taverner's Trust (cricket)[7], the Golf Foundation[8] and several other charitable bodies. Sportsmatch was a scheme launched by the Government in 1992 which will be considered in more detail when we look at sources of potential revenue funding.

The Foundation for Sport and the Arts

The Foundation for Sport and the Arts[9] was set up in 1990 by the Football Pools companies as an alternative to a National Lottery. The pools companies put £40 million into the Foundation per annum and the Government £20 million through offering offering a 2.5% reduction in the rate of Pool Betting Duty. Chaired by Tim Rice, with Grattan Endicott as Secretary, the Foundation prides itself on having no set criteria for distributing funds. There has been some criticism of this attitude, as it means that little account is taken of funds given by other bodies such as the appropriate local authority or the Sports Council. On the other hand, organisations that have received grants are very grateful for any support, and £60 million is a great deal of money to go into sport and the arts. In the first year of its existence, the foundation awarded 486 grants and this number probably doubled in the second year. Small community sport and leisure projects, of a type which would never receive any attention from other organisations, have been the recipients of grants. As an example, the small village of Billesdon in Leicestershire, with a population of around 1,000 people, received £50,000 from the Foundation which will be used for a new £300,000 recreation centre. A new village sports facility will include a main hall, space for two badminton courts, changing facilities and a meeting room. There is no doubt that the Foundation is making a real contribution to sport and art in the UK and it is rather a pity that their contribution is not given the respect it deserves.

The three year agreement with the Government is due to expire in 1995, but it is expected that the Charter will be renewed. Funding from the Foundation will therefore be available alongside that from the National Lottery.

The National Lottery

Looking to the future, provision for sport, particularly with the public and voluntary sectors, is likely to be transformed by funds from the National Lottery. Most of 1994 will be spent in discussing, offering and awarding the contract to run the Lottery, but all being well, the Lottery should begin at the end of 1994, or at the latest at the beginning of 1995 and funds will begin to flow into sport soon after that.

The National Lottery Act was enacted in October 1993. It states that five bodies will be responsible for distributing the funds for charities, the arts, sport, heritage and a newly established Millennium Fund. Each body would receive 20 per cent of the funds available for distribution and for sport this distribution would be split as follows:

The Sports Council	83.3%
The Scottish Sports Council	8.9%
The Sports Council for Wales	5.0%
The Sports Council for Northern Ireland	2.8%

This split has been calculated in direct proportion to the population of each country named.

It is calculated that the National Lottery could have a turnover of £4 billion a year. Taxation announced by the Treasury will be 12 per cent, with prizes expected to take up about 48-52 per cent. Operating costs are expected to be between 12-15 per cent of the turnover, which leaves 23-30 per cent available for distribution to good causes. It is therefore estimated that the sum available for distribution for sport will quickly rise to £100 million per annum with the potential to rise to a figure as high as £200 million per annum in years to come. When Peter Davis, Director-General of the National Lottery, announced details of the licence to operate the lottery, it was made clear that applicants will be expected to show a "decreasing percentage of turnover spent on administration costs" as turnover increases, thus "maximising the proportion of turnover to be distributed to good causes". A share of proceeds from television rights and other ancillary merchandising will be returned to good causes.

In preparation for the introduction of the National Lottery in the UK, David Carpenter, now Head of the National Lottery Planning team at the Sports Council, carried out extensive research into existing lotteries in the EC. In various briefings he has highlighted that turnover in EC Europe and the Nordic countries of Norway, Sweden and Finland account for an annual turnover of £15 billion out of a world-wide turnover of £38 billion in 1991. In Scandinavia, the Lottery was originally based on the Football Pools, but other products have been added in the past 10 years. In 1991, lottery income for sport ranged between £37 million and £58.6 million, and this is in countries whose average population is 4-5 million. Lottery funds have acted as a catalyst for major initiatives such as the preparation for the Winter Olympic Games at Lillehammer in 1994 and elite programmes like 'Team Danmark'. There has to be a connection between the success of various international Scandinavian teams and the lottery funding, although the Lottery is also used to promote the development of schemes at a local level, particularly in partnership with the voluntary sector.

The lottery industry is based around four products. Passive draws (like raffle tickets, already used widely by charities in this country); Instant/Scratch Games like the cards you are often given at petrol stations; Lotto and the football pools. Based on these different types of games, the per capita sales on Lottery products in 1991, showed the highest spend was in Norway where £2.21 per annum was spent per head of population. If you take the nationally marketed products which already exist in the UK, like the football pools etc., then our spend per head is £0.26 per week. However, if you look at all gambling in the UK, which takes in betting, bingo, casinos etc., then the UK tops the poll. On average, each person in the UK spends £4.45 each week on gambling, which is higher than any other country in the world.

No one really knows what effect the introduction of the National Lottery will have on gambling in the UK. From experience from other countries, it would appear that the football pools are most vulnerable, followed by charity scratch card games marketed on a wider than local basis. There is no clear evidence world-wide to support that other forms of gambling are affected, although many parts of the industry have their own ideas of the effects on their business. For example, the betting shop industry are expecting a 5 per cent drop in their takings. It is hoped that any loss experienced by charities will be made up by the proportion of funds distributed to charities from the Lottery. There is an argument that our football culture is so ingrained in this country, that the pools will suffer little as a result of the introduction of the Lottery. Until the Lottery has been up and running for some years, no one will really know what effect it will have.

A note of caution in this area has to be sounded when looking at the distribution of funds from the National Lottery in the Republic of Ireland. In Ireland, a National Lottery was introduced in 1987 and funds have been used for a five year programme for facilities at national regional and local level. The most significant change in policy in Ireland is the number of added beneficiaries who now receive funding from the Lottery. When the scheme was first launched, 55 per cent of funds were destined for sport and recreational facilities, with arts and culture benefiting from the remainder. By 1991, other beneficiaries had been added, such as health and welfare, support for youth and recreation and the Irish language. An article in a national newspaper suggested that the real reason why a National Sports Centre had not been built as planned at Custom Dock in Dublin was that "the Department of Finance saw how easy it was to siphon off Lotto money to prop up any government shortfall".

In the UK, the Government has made it clear that all funding from the National Lottery will be additional to existing grants. In other words, The Sports Council grant-in-aid of £50 million in 1993-94 will remain fairly constant, dropping to £48 million in 1996-97, with the shortfall being made up by increased efficiency.

In November 1993, Iain Sproat MP, the Parliamentary Under Secretary at the Department of National Heritage, speaking at a conference[10] made a number of useful pronouncements. Firstly he made it clear that:

"Government intends National Lottery funds to be additional, so that they make a real impact and enable projects to go ahead which might otherwise not have found funds. The Government will not make any case by case reduction in conventional expenditure programmes to take account of awards from the Lottery."

He went on to say that the distribution bodies will publish guidance specifying the criteria for eligibility of Lottery proceeds, but that some basic principles had been well established. These included:

"The emphasis will be on capital facilities that would not otherwise be provided at national, regional and local level. We believe that the prospect of such capital sums from the Lottery will encourage public/private sector partnerships"

"Priority will be given to applications which have a partnership funding element. This could include, for example, a local authority paying for the running costs and the private sector putting in a capital contribution, to enable a good mix of more commercial activities to balance the less commercial activities funded by the Lottery."

At the time of writing it looks as if revenue support for projects will only be considered in exceptional circumstances and that applicants will normally have to demonstrate how revenue costs will be covered on an ongoing basis.

From the private sector perspective, it is hoped that the National Lottery will achieve a number of aims. There is much sense is using some of the expertise which exists in the private sector to ensure that the best use is made of funds from the National Lottery and that tight control is placed on project management. Private sector experience in consultancy for large projects, quantity surveying, project management, architecture and construction should be utilised by the applicants to ensure best value for money. **There is a real opportunity for partnership between the public and private sectors which should not be missed.**

Secondly, there are obviously projects which will benefit from a mixture of Lottery fund and private sector capital. One can imagine that local authorities bidding for funds from the Lottery will be required to find some of the funding, perhaps 50 per cent, themselves. As we turn to look next at the what the private sector has to offer, it should be possible to identify what type of assistance the private sector can and will offer.

In the history of sport and of partnership, the National Lottery offers a great opportunity for the 1990s. It will create new 'state of the art' facilities for the youth of tomorrow, which will encourage participation and train our world and Olympic champions of the future. If used wisely, funds from the Lottery will allow us to continue the tradition of facilities provided with funding from the public sector, which are available to everyone to use whatever their means. It will not however be the answer to everything. In their strategy 'Sport in the Nineties — New Horizons', The Sports Council list their requirements for the funding of national and specialist facilities for a ten year programme. The cost of this programme is estimated at £1,700 million, with community facilities costing another £2,250 million. If implemented, this programme would swallow up all the funds from the National Lottery and more for the next ten years. The funds from the National Lottery begin to look like a drop in the ocean, which is why the private sector will still have such an important part to play.

Notes and references

1. *'Sport in the Nineties: New Horizons'* — published by the Sports Council, 16 Upper Woburn Place, London WC1H 0QP, — 071 388 1277. Price £10.

2. The Institute of Sport and Recreation Management (ISRM) — 0664 65531.

3. *'Brussels in focus: EC Access for Sport'* by Bill Seary in co-operation with the International Affairs Unit of the Sports Council, 1992, available from the Sports Council £10.

4. English Partnerships — see chapter 2, note 3.

5. The Football Trust — 071 388 4504.

6. The Lawn Tennis Foundation — The Lawn Tennis Association, 071 385 2366.

7. The Lord Taverner's Trust — 071 222 0707.

8. The Golf Foundation — 0920 484044.

9. The Foundation for Sport and the Arts, PO Box 666, Liverpool L69 7JN — 051 524 0235/6.

10. Speech by Iain Sproat at the BISL Annual Conference November 1993, available from BISL.

The growth of the private sector and a definition of partners

The next two chapters will examine the private sector, what it comprises and how to define potential partners. This will be followed by a look at different types of partnership and where the private sector is interested in investing. So what do we mean by the private sector? Who are these potential partners and how can they be contacted? As we have seen in Chapter 3, the first private sector companies to provide funding for schemes like the Coral Reef at Bracknell were property developers. So let us begin with an assessment of property developers and their potential as partners for local authorities.

Property developers

The 1980s was the time of the property developer. Rosehaugh, Stanhope, Brookmount, Citygrove, Carter Commercial, Capital and Counties, St Modwen, Imry Merchant Developers, Arlington, and Clayform. There were many others; some of which still exist, but many of whom have disappeared, or are now much smaller organisations.

In simplistic terms, property development works in three ways. The developer may be building something for which he is looking for tenants, but intends to keep as a long term investment. Perhaps one of the most successful property developers in this country is Land Securities and many of their developments are managed on this basis. Secondly, a developer may be looking to develop a site for which he has already tied up the tenants, but intends to sell on the freehold to tenants or to institutional funding as soon as he can. Thirdly, a site may be developed as a speculative investment. In this latter case, the developer takes a gamble on the likely demand by tenants and hopes that he can walk away at the end with a profit.

During the 1980s, a number of property developers became interested in leisure. In some cases, their interest was driven by the development brief produced by the local authority, who demanded a mixed-use scheme, or the property developer themselves decided that leisure was an important component of their proposed development. If the scheme was devised by the property developer and taken to the planning authority without any invitation from the council, then the inclusion of sport and leisure facilities might make it more acceptable. At the end of the day, whichever way it worked, the local authority would end up with commercial leisure as part of a mixed use scheme and, if they owned the land, a capital receipt to be used how they liked. This is how the Bracknell scheme worked. The Council put together a development brief for a mixed use of the site and following a developer competition, which was won by Peel Investments, an agreed capital sum was paid to the Council for the land. It was then up to the local authority to decide how to spend this money and at Bracknell they decided to use the capital for the development of the Coral Reef Leisure Pool.

In some cases, a retail scheme without any form of leisure was used to generate a capital receipt. In Watford, the Harlequinns shopping centre was developed by Capital and Counties on land owned by Watford Borough Council. No leisure existed as part of the retail scheme, but the Council used the receipt to pay for the Watford Springs swimming pool. Of course, this was before the implementation of the 50% rule, so the Council was able to use the whole receipt to pay for the pool. Many smaller sports development were provided on this basis. With the development boom in the 1980s even small rural authorities found themselves with property developers looking to develop sites in their area which would generate a capital receipt.

There is a difference between a developer who is primarily interested in developing retail, offices or housing and includes leisure because it is a good add-on or because the development brief demands it and a developer who is putting together a pure leisure scheme. Just as the 1980s saw the appearance of out-of-town and edge-of-town shopping centres, so it also saw the appearance of similar developments which were purely leisure based. These schemes were often on the edge of town, with a building area of some 100,000 sq ft and about 700 car parking spaces. Facilities were provided to attract families and parties with differing age groups. Some schemes were designed with a mixture of commercial leisure (ten-pin bowling, cinema, nightclub and restaurants) and 'quasi sport' facilities like leisure ice. Several local authorities demanded such a mix. Other schemes, like the Carter Commercial Developments project at Shawridge Leisure Park, Swindon, were purely commercial leisure developments. It is probably fair to say that schemes which included just commercial leisure facilities were easier to put together. The Shawridge park contains an MGM 8 screen multiplex cinema, 36 lane Super Bowl, 1,000 capacity nightclub, Pizza Hut restaurant, pub/diner and cafe/bar. It is co-incidentally situated on the opposite side of the road to the local authority owned Links Leisure centre.

Two leisure schemes which did include 'sport' facilities were developed in Stoke-on-Trent and in Poole, Dorset. In Stoke-on-Trent, St Modwen Developments put together the winning bid for the regeneration of the site of the Stoke-on-Trent Garden Festival, once the Garden Festival was over. A business and light industrial park is complemented by a commercial leisure development, which has a multiplex cinema, ten-pin bowl, waterworld, ski slope, amusements and a variety of restaurants. In Poole, Tower Park, on the edge of town, was developed by WH White. In addition to commercial leisure, a significant part of which is operated by Allied Leisure Plc, whose headquarters is at Tower Park, it also includes a leisure ice rink and leisure pool.

The potential for these property developers to provide investment for local authority sport and leisure changes and has changed over the past five years. If we consider that during the 1980s property developers were at their most active, then the beginning of the 1990s has seen little activity. The recession and the drop in land values hit the property developer hardest and many schemes that received outline planning permission never went ahead. Town centre redevelopments in places like Hastings and Durham were shelved and therefore sport and leisure projects, which rested either on a developers plans to include them, or on the capital receipt which the local authority was going to use for its own sport and leisure plans, failed to come to fruition. Sport and leisure facilities are the 'bête noire' of the property developer. On one hand they make a mixed-use scheme more attractive, both to planning authorities and to people that use them, and on the other hand the rents that they are likely to attract make them a lost leader and if the plan is only just viable, the less commercial elements, i.e sport and leisure facilities, are dropped.

On a more positive note, as the UK emerges from the recession in the 1990s and development activity increases once more, there is plenty of scope for property developers to provide either a planning gain or a capital receipt, which a council can use for its own purposes. Inevitably, economic growth in the 1990s will see the resurgence of the property developer and therefore the ability for them to act as potential partners should not be dismissed. Although we are unlikely to return to the property boom years of the 1980s, this does not mean that property development will cease altogether.

For the local authority there are a number of issues to bear in mind when considering the plans of property developers. If the local authority is setting out the brief for a particular site and wishes to include sport and leisure in the scheme, then it should say so from the start. If the site is very large and very commercial, it may well be possible to include sport facilities as well as commercial leisure and in chapter 6, we will consider a case study of the Hemel Hempstead site, which illustrates this point. Beware of other departments who may have other ideas! There are several potential leisure developments which have gone awry because the transport department insisted on expensive alterations to roads which took away any value left for a sport development. Coventry City Council hoped to refurbish its sports centre through the re-development of an adjoining site. By the time other departments in the council had insisted on a new bus station, the site had reduced to a negative value and competing facilities had been developed in nearby Rugby. In fact, in the end the scheme became totally unviable and never went ahead. The council has been left with little option but to pay itself for the redevelopment of the sports centre which contains two 50m pools.

If the property developer comes to the local authority with a proposal, then the planning department needs to be sure that if sport and leisure facilities are needed in the area, they can then use the opportunity to secure these facilities in the proposed scheme. Again the relationship between the leisure department and the planning or development department is crucial. The leisure department should identify what facilities are needed, both for sport and for commercial leisure. It can then play a proactive role in ensuring that the planning department knows what type of investment is needed in this area. If the leisure department is proactive, it is more likely that part of a capital receipt will be earmarked for sport development. A strong Chief Executive or Chief Leisure Officer will ensure that sport has a greater influence.

Consider every potential developer as a potential provider of some sort of capital for investment for council owned sport and leisure centres. No doubt the leisure department will have their work cut out to persuade other members of the council that sport and leisure is the priority, which is why it is worth leisure departments being proactive in attracting developers to the area. Consider good commercial leisure facilities as important as good sport facilities. Obviously capital receipts and planning gains raised from commercial leisure operators are more likely to find their way into sport, particularly if the operators were attracted to the area by the leisure department.

Owner-operators

This brings us on to our second category of partner. Quite apart from the difference between types of developer, there is also a difference between a developer and an owner operator. A developer in all probability has no interest in operating any of the facilities which appear on the site. An owner-operator often takes space from a developer, but is also prepared to act on his own. If the site is very large, then it is inevitable that a developer will be needed to act as a lead. Few individual owner-operators are prepared to take on major ground works or highways work before occupying a site. They would much rather let a developer do the preparatory work and then take over space which can be made operational within 18 months. On smaller sites, many commercial leisure facilities can be stand-alone, and the operator will deal directly with the landowner to buy the site. The important thing about owner-operators is that they are buying land to develop their own facilities which they will then keep. Owner-operators include[1]:

Allied Leisure Plc	Grand Metropolitan Estates
Archer Leisure (formerly Queens Moat Leisure)	Bass Leisure
Forte	Ogden Entertainment Services
Garfunkels Restaurants	Allied Breweries
Boddingtons Plc	McDonalds
Bright Reasons	National Leisure Catering
The Brent Walker Group Plc	Compass Services
The Broadgate Club Plc	European Leisure
Carden Park	Northern Leisure
David Lloyd Leisure Plc	UCI (UK)
First Leisure Corporation	Warner Bros Theatres
Granada Group Plc	Rank Leisure

Greenalls Inns   Scottish & Newcastle Plc
Whitbread Plc   Wates Leisure
Wembley Plc   Mansfield Brewery Plc
ISL Leisure

It is important to distinguish between local authorities who in the main operate sports facilities such as swimming pools, ice rinks, sports halls, health clubs and sports pitches and private sector owner-operators who operate commercial leisure facilities. Certain facilities operated by local authorities are now also operated as commercial leisure facilities — health and squash clubs are good examples of this. There are also some facilities which, in the 1970s and early 1980s, would only have been managed by private sector companies such as ten-pin bowling and nightclubs, which are now included in local authority schemes. In general terms, it should be noted that the private sector represents a huge capacity for investment across a wide sphere of activities. As a general guide owner-operators of commercial leisure facilities are broadly interested in developing facilities under the following headings:

Ten Pin Bowling   Theme Parks
Bingo   Golf Courses
Amusements   Indoor Tennis Centres
Motorway Service Stations   Hotels
Health and Fitness   Cinemas
Marinas   Betting Shops
Pubs   Snooker
Restaurants   Holiday Centres

In the 1980s, owner–operators of commercial leisure were on the whole fairly quiet. Whilst the sale of land for property development was booming, land was too expensive for commercial leisure. Large owner operators like First Leisure concentrated on keeping their gearing (borrowings) as low as possible. Some of the smaller operators like Whitegate Leisure and European Leisure who tried to expand too quickly came unstuck and are only just recovering, whilst companies like Leisure Investments disappeared altogether.

The 1990s has seen a fall in land prices which for leisure developments means that prices are now much more realistic. As development for retail and offices has virtually come to a standstill, then leisure operators have been there to buy sites and expand. Leisure is fashionable and therefore very fickle. In the 1930s, ten-pin bowling saw an expansion, it them became unpopular and sites died. In the late 1980s and 1990s the advent of auto scoring, offering managers computerised records of user figures rather than having to rely on staff reports has made ten-pin bowling popular again and it has since seen enormous growth. The emergence of the multiplex cinema which offers three, six or ten films on one site with comfortable seats and excellent sound and vision systems has transformed the size of the cinema audience in this country — in 1993, cinema admissions have been estimated at 112 million. One of the greatest difficulties for the leisure industry of the introduction of five year Local, Structure and UDP Plans is that leisure is so fashion conscious. Already some operators believe that ten-pin bowling has reached saturation point. Additional attractions like Quasar and other laser games are being added to ten-pin bowling centres, and obviously this needs to be taken into account by planning authorities identifying suitable sites. Much can happen to the leisure market in five years. David Lloyd has pioneered the growth in commercial indoor tennis and health centres and has opened eight in the last ten years. This has been matched by the Indoor Tennis Initiative from the Lawn Tennis Association (which is jointly funded by the Sports Council and the All-England Lawn Tennis Club). There are strong signs that several of the major owner-operators are moving into the health and fitness market. First Leisure now own 75 per cent of ISL Leisure, who developed the Royal Berkshire Racquet and Croquet Club in Bracknell. Local plans must take changes in leisure into account and need to be aware of the flexibility required in their plans to accommodate changes in leisure fashions.

Owner–operators of commercial leisure make very good partners for local authorities. We will look in the next chapter at the type of sites operators are looking for, but there is an obvious synergy in placing certain types of commercial leisure facilities next to traditional sports facilities. As we have already considered at Crowtree in Sunderland, having facilities to suit all age groups which offer both passive and active types of sport and leisure on one site will attract more visitors and attract them to repeat their visit. A good mix of sport and leisure facilities in a area is important to attract new industry and buyers for homes. How many times do you read a development brief, tourist booklet, or any other type of prospectus in an area which specifically mentions the breadth of sport and leisure facilities available in that location. This is seen as a good reason to visit, relocate offices or live there.

This is why leisure departments need to understand the leisure market as well as they do the sports market. Sports facilities may be directly in their remit, but they need balanced leisure provision and if a capital receipt or planning gain is going to come from a commercial leisure operator, then the proceeds are much more likely to find their way into sports provision.

As a general guide, leisure facilities which are likely to raise the largest site premiums are in order of value, as follows:

Multi-screen cinema
Fast food (hamburger)
Themed restaurant
Ten-pin bowling
Fast food (Pizza)
Pub steak house
Nightclub
Speciality restaurant
Cafe bar
Roadside cafe
Bingo
Snooker

Hotel operators also make good partners, but obviously their value is calculated on a premium per acre.

This list is very general and intended to be only a guide. Obviously the location, population and catchment of an area will alter the attractiveness of the site.

Sites for owner–operators

Perhaps the most difficult assessment which a local authority has to make is whether the site they are considering is likely to be of interest to private sector leisure operators. In November 1993, a document titled 'Planning for Commercial Leisure'[2] was published to give a clearer understanding of site criteria for these facilities. This booklet presents an attempt by the private sector to create a better understanding of planning for commercial leisure. It acknowledges that the Sports Council and its regional offices ensure that the needs of sport are well known and understood by planning authorities. The English Tourist Board and the regional Tourist Boards perform a similar function for tourism and it is to their credit that many local authorities have sustainable tourism strategies in areas without obvious tourism potential.

The document gives guidelines on the criteria governing suitable sites for 19 different types of leisure facility, from amusement arcade to bingo, from hotels with leisure facilities to motorway services, from multiplex cinemas to nightclubs, from pubs to restaurants and from stadia to indoor tennis centres. Each facility has the following headings; types of facility; location (including its position in relation to motorways or major roads and its population catchment area); size of site; car parking requirements (number of spaces); building height; building type (e.g. traditional, brick etc.); employment created; operating (is the business seasonal and when is it open?); and will give examples of a typical development.

It is not the place of this book to replicate the details of the 'Planning for Commercial Leisure' Document, but the following chart gives some idea of the location and size of commercial leisure facilities covered in this document.

Facility	Location	Size of Building
Amusement Centre	Town Centre/Seaside Resort	1,500 to 5,000 sq ft
Bingo and Social Club	Towns with populations of 50–70,000 plus	25,000 to 35,000 sq ft (1.5–2 acres)
Budget Hotel	Motorway/trunk road	15,000 sq ft per floor (1.5 to 2 acres)
Country Hotel	100,000 people within 15 minutes	96,000 sq ft, (175 acres)
Hotel with Leisure 15 minutes	155,000 people within	90,000 sq ft (5 acres)
Indoor Tennis	Edge of Town	12,000 sq ft (8 acres)
Motorway Service Area	Adjacent to motorway	Site 20 acres upwards
Multi-Leisure complex	Catchment of 500,000 plus	100,000 sq ft (10 acres)
Nightclub: 1,600 to 1,800 capacity	Edge of Town, population over 100,000	20-25,000 sq ft (1.5–3 acre)
Nightclub 800 to 1,000 capacity	Town centre, population over 50,000	10–15,000 sq ft (1 acre)
Public House	Off town centre locations or high streets in smaller towns	1,500 to 4,000 sq ft
Pub Restaurant	Main arterial roads from town centre or attractive destination locations	8,000 sq ft (1–3 acres)
Licensed Restaurant	Good secondary/primary high street or free-standing on retail or leisure park, or main road	1,500 to 2,000 sq ft or out of town 0.4/0.5 acre
Destination Restaurant	High Street locations, or prominent major roads	8,000 sq ft or out of town 1.5–2 acres
Multi-Purpose stadia 20–25,000 seats	Edge of Town – 1 million within 1 hour	9 - 20 acres
Stadia Complex 60–80,000 seats	5–15 miles from major city centre	30-60 acres
Ten-Pin Bowling	Towns with population over 150,000	30–50,000 sq ft (2–3 acres)

In subsequent chapters we will look at the employment created by these facilities.

By the mid-1990s, the whole of the UK will be governed by UDP, Local and Structure Plans. Through lack of understanding, many local authorities have failed to include good sites for commercial leisure in their plans and as already pointed out, five year reviews create a long period of waiting. Some of the larger owner-operators are scouring the country and commenting on every plan in areas where they are interested in developing in the future. The cost of this is enormous and beyond most middle sized or small companies. Once again the leisure department and indeed the planning department has a role to play in making sure that suitable sites for leisure are identified in their local plan.

Owner-operators outside the leisure sector

There is obviously some potential for partnership with other owner-operators who do not fall under the heading of the commercial leisure sector. Probably the most obvious type of operator who does not always use a developer are the supermarket chains. The relationship between shopping and leisure will be examined in chapter 5. Suffice to say at this stage that it is unlikely that supermarket operators will be interested in developing sport and leisure facilities to be used by customers coming to shop. However, supermarkets have high commercial values. Therefore their potential for providing planning gain and capital receipts is huge. Even small communities need to be able to shop for food and whether you believe that it is a good thing or not, supermarkets have taken over the role of many corner shops. A new swimming pool opened in 1991 at Wells provided by Mendip Borough Council was paid for from a capital receipt from the sale of land to a supermarket. There are many other examples of this type of partnership, but Wells happens to be a good example, as it is the smallest city in the UK!

Construction companies

Construction companies can make good partners for sport and leisure developments and are increasingly interested in funding their own construction work in return for a contract. At the end of 1993, Construction Forecast and Research Ltd is predicting that the construction industry will show a slight drop in activity from the low reached at the end of 1992. As margins are cut and as companies compete against each other, not only has the cost of construction decreased, but most of the major contractors will attempt 'financial engineering' in an effort to attract new projects.

In Manchester, Bovis Construction is raising the funds to construct the new Velodrome. The funds are loaned through a bank, with Bovis, or its parent company, P&O, acting as guarantor. At the end of the construction phase, the cost will be repaid, along with any interest, by Vector, the company set up to channel the mix of public and private sector funding for this project.

Public sector partners

Another category of partner for a local authority looking at sport and leisure comes under the category of other public sector organisations. Changes to the National Health Service have created trusts and self-funding hospitals that can make very good partners for local authorities. NHS hospitals and other institutions are often large land holders and in some cases owners of parks or sport and leisure facilities for their medical staff. Chapters 6 considers a couple of case studies where partnership arrangements for the benefit of sport have arisen from partnerships with NHS organisations. Similarly, many educational establishments are now self-funding. They may own sports centres, but they also have large student populations which need accommodation. There are some good examples of local authorities who have obtained planning gains or sold land to NHS or educational establishments for student accommodation. Often a developer or construction company is prepared to fund such developments when there is a 'sitting tenant' in the number of students requiring accommodation when the project is completed.

Turning to revenue funding, there are also opportunities for partnership with the NHS through GP Referral schemes. We will look at examples of how this works in chapter 8.

Compulsory Competitive Tendering (CCT)

The introduction of CCT has thrown up a new set of partners. As the local authority becomes the client, his contractor is likely to be one of three different types of potential partners. The first is the Direct Service Organisation (DSO). In most instances they are investors in reducing the deficit funding from the council, but ideas are surfacing for DSOs to become investors in capital programmes too. More obvious partners under CCT legislation are Management Buy-Outs (MBOs) or private sector contractors. Probably the best known management buyout team was at St Albans, where the Director of Leisure, John McGinley, now runs Relaxion Leisure Group Plc. MBOs become private sector companies and therefore should be grouped as potential partners with private sector companies operating in this area. When we look at CCT in chapter 7, we will see the potential for reducing revenue funding and for capital investment from these companies.

Summary

This rather basic definition of the partners available for sport and leisure projects is deliberately simplified. The headings given often become blurred, but to summarise, partners may be:

- **Developers:**
  - Interested in sport and leisure as a component of a mixed-use scheme
  - Can be encouraged to include sport and leisure facilities in their scheme, or to provide a planning gain
  - Are purely interested in leisure development
- **Owner-Operators**
  - Will develop commercial leisure and possibly sports facilities
  - Will develop commercial leisure adjacent to sports centres, thereby providing a capital receipt
  - This chapter summaries the type of facilities owner operators are interested in developing
  - Gives an idea of the commercial leisure facilities most likely to raise the largest premiums
  - Looks at the catchment and size of site required
- **Construction Companies**
  - Possible investors in sport and leisure facilities
- **Public Sector**
  - Possible partnerships from Educational Establishments and the NHS
- **CCT Operators**
  - Potential partners for capital and revenue investment

It is important to understand the distinction between a developer who is primarily interested in retail, offices or housing who can become interested in leisure if this idea is put into his mind and the developer who is interested and knowledgeable about commercial leisure developments. Similarly, it is important to understand the difference between a developer who walks away from the project at the end of the day and an owner-operator who is interested in buying land to keep.

Finally, it is important to understand the potential for involving the construction industry, other public sector organisations and CCT operators in generating capital and revenue funding for sport and leisure facilities.

If these are the partners, where are they interested in developing?

Notes and references

1. A list of owner-operators who are members of BISL can be obtained from BISL.

2. *'Planning for Commercial Leisure'*, Published by BISL, price £15.

5

Where is the private sector interested in developing and what type of partnerships are we seeking to define

So, if the last chapter identified the potential partners, where is the private sector interested in investing? What potential has a local authority for attracting investment in its geographical area and within that area are leisure operators interested in locations in-town, out-of town, or on the edge-of-town? Let us begin by looking at the synergy of sport and leisure with other types of development. This will provide an indication of their potential as partners for sport and leisure facilities.

Shopping and leisure

There was much debate in the 1980s about the value of shopping and leisure. Ideas came thick and fast from across the Atlantic where several huge shopping and leisure developments opened. The most famous was probably West Edmonton Mall in Canada which is a huge amusement park with leisure pool, rides and every conceivable type of leisure activity, alongside an equally huge shopping mall. Discussion surrounding the concept of shopping and leisure concentrated on whether the leisure created a destination visit, whether it was just an add on, or indeed whether it was a perhaps a distraction. There were also many arguments about the value of stripping off for a swim in a leisure pool, while the contents of the shopping brought in the supermarket deteriorated in the back of the car!

There is no doubt that West Edmonton Mall was a destination visit. In other words people went there to use the leisure facilities in their own right — it was the main reason for their visit. They may also have gone with shopping as the main reason for their visit. Whatever the reason, both the shopping and the leisure were attractions large enough to stand alone, but also to be complementary. Once there, visitors who went for the shops found themselves participating in the leisure and vice versa. At the end of the visit they found they did not have enough time to do everything and so returned on another occasion, so creating that all important repeat visit.

According to Mark Potiriadis of S&P, if the leisure takes up more than 25 per cent of the retail space, then it creates a destination in its own right. If the leisure is less than 10 per cent then it is just an added enhancement, but was not large enough to attract visits for its own sake. In this country leisure in shopping centres tends to be passive, rather than active. Leisure tends to be located in edge-of-town, or out-of-town shopping centres which often include multiplex cinemas, ten-pin bowling and nightclubs. Sometimes there is a health club, but rarely sports halls or a swimming pool.

Probably one of the best known edge-of-town shopping centres in the UK is the Metrocentre at Gateshead. Developed by Sir John Hall, it was then taken over by the Church Commissioners and it has become a destination visit for millions of visitors from all over the country. The leisure developed more by accident than design, but it is large enough to be a destination in its own right. Metroland is a children's play ground, developed on American lines. It is interesting that when it was opened it was found that culturally its use was very different from an equivalent area in North America. It was designed as somewhere where parents could leave their children, but in the north east that never happened and seating had to be installed for parents to sit on to watch their children play. The Metrocentre contains several foodcourts, ten-pin bowling and a health club. It is interesting to note that when the multiplex cinema opened, sales in teenage fashion shops increased by 15 per cent because the same people who came to the cinema visited the fashion shops. In a smaller shopping centre like Whiteleys in Queensway in London, the opening of the cinema had less of an effect on the customer for the shops. Whiteleys has a range of up-market fashion shops. Their clientele is rather different from the youngsters who go to the cinema. However, although the number of visitors to the shops did not increase when the cinema opened, the turnover of the food court situated outside the cinema doubled. The combination of a visit to the cinema, proceeded or followed by a meal was an obvious attraction.

In developing shopping centres with commercial leisure attached, some understanding must be made of possible conflicts. Opening hours for leisure go beyond 8 pm, when the shopping centre is likely to shut, unless retailers believe that window shopping is important to their trade. Often it is necessary to provide a special car park and entrance for the leisure facilities. At the Liberty II Centre in Romford, where Trafalgar House developed a shopping centre with a Rank Organisation commercial leisure development above, specially reinforced ceilings had to cope with the weight loads demanded by the leisure. There were problems with noise penetration from the nightclub to the cinema. Schemes like this can and do work, but it is well to be aware of the potential problems from the start.

Many people would argue that all shopping is a leisure activity — although many men and women known to us all would probably disagree! It really depends on your reason for shopping. Firstly, there is shopping for a specific purpose. You go to buy food or for a particular item from the particular shop. Even the large supermarkets chains disagree about whether you will look for other items when the purpose of your visit is to buy food. Sainsburys and Safeway offer little else other than food, while Asda and Tesco have clothing and other items. There are some sports centres which are next to superstores in this country, like the Norwich Sports Village, but the connection (as noted in the last chapter), is more likely to be a planning gain than a genuine belief that people who go to shop for food are also interested in taking part in a sport or leisure activity.

It is more likely that you will find leisure facilities in shopping centres where they are offering 'comparative shopping'. In other words you set out to buy a shirt and you are wanting to compare the choice and the price of shirts in a variety of shops. After all, this is probably what town centre shopping is all about, which is the traditional home for sport and leisure activities. Although as noted in the introduction to this section, most shopping centres with leisure facilities contain passive commercial leisure facilities, with the exception of a health club, there are a couple of examples where more active sporting pursuits have been added. Perhaps one of the most comprehensive and successful shopping and retail schemes to be built in the UK in recent years is the shopping centre at East Kilbride in Scotland.

Developed through a partnership between the Urban Development Corporation and Land Securities, the 270,000 sq ft shopping centre has at its centre a full sized ice-rink. This scheme defies any argument about the distraction value of leisure in a shopping centre and according to the Development Corporation has contributed to the overall success of the scheme where the retail is fully let. Quite apart from the ice rink there is also a UCI multiplex cinema, nightclub, foodcourt and video wall. The Development Corporation admit that they are still having problems in finding independent operators to take on the ice rink, without offering any revenue support, despite the popularity of ice in Scotland and the inclusion of curling lanes. East Kilbride is a new town with a population of around 2,000 people, but very much on the edge of Glasgow with very good motorway links. It is a good example of a shopping and leisure scheme, but it also a good example of the part played by Urban Development Corporations and Commissions for New Towns in devising and encouraging imaginative partnership arrangements which include sport and leisure facilities. There is no doubt that these organisations appreciate the importance of sport and leisure in the lives of their local communities and are determined to ensure that new towns are adequately provided with these facilities.

In-town versus out-of-town

Just as there has been endless discussion about the merits of shopping and leisure developments, there has equally been discussion about the merits of developing sport and leisure facilities in-town or on the edge of town. Many of the large mixed-use commercial leisure schemes covered above have been on the edge of town. The Metrocentre in Gateshead, Meadowland in Sheffield and Merry Hill in Dudley have all been edge-of-town sites which contained commercial leisure facilities and in all three cities, the town centre has suffered a decline.

The past five years have seen a move towards edge-of-town stand alone leisure developments for ten-pin bowling, nightclubs and many restaurants that are considered destination visits. This is often because prime city centre retail space is generally too expensive to be attractive to leisure operators and many older city centre shopping centres lack the space to accommodate leisure in any form. The need for car parking is often an additional problem. On edge-of-town sites, facilities like ten-pin bowling have been moving into disused carpet-warehouses.

Now that the property boom of the 1980s is over, many local authorities are making a great effort to attract leisure back to the town centre. These authorities can acquire sites and help with grant applications. Encouragement for in-town developments is very much a priority for the Department of Environment. Towns like Luton and Maidstone which successfully fought off attempts by developers to put in leisure facilities on out-of-town sites are now trying hard to put together sites to attract developers in town. According to a Leisure Week 'Review of Property', THI Developments has been given consent to develop a multiplex, nightclub and bingo centre on a 2.5 acre site in the centre of Luton. There is also some political pressure for this trend. A Planning Policy Guidance Note (PPG 13) issued by the Department for Transport, states that local authorities should not encourage schemes which require private transport. Many organisations argued that the problems of car pollution should be more easily be dealt with by car manufacturers than by restrictions on land use.

In recent pronouncements on the subject, the Department of the Environment has been keen to support innovative design, but has rejected several applications for out-of-town retail development. This view will in time have an affect on the leisure industry too. However, it remains to be seen whether central and local government succeed in encouraging leisure operators to occupy town centre sites.

Leisure in office developments

Several office developments have included sports centres, mainly in the form of a health club. In Milton Keynes, a large health club is operated by LivingWell as part of a 250,000 sq ft office block, very close to the shopping centre. The developer saw the inclusion of space for a health club as a means of letting the office space. Many of the large London office developments such as the Broadgate Centre and the Royal Mint include a health club. The important factor is that office workers will use these facilities during their lunch break and at the beginning and end of the day. There has also been a growth in recent years in office tenants providing their own corporate health and fitness facilities. There is ample evidence that these facilities decrease the number of days which staff take off sick. Most corporate health centres will be staffed by a physiotherapist, so that the treatment for back or neck pain, that would have meant that a member of staff had a day off sick, can be treated on the premises. Personnel directors will see staff morale rise with the inclusion of health facilities in the building. Even if fitness is not the main reason for using it, health and weight loss often attract staff who otherwise would have little aptitude or reason to visit a health club near their home.

Leisure and housing developments

In the 1980s, many housing developers sought to include a health club, small community swimming pool or sports centre in new housing developments. Just as office developments saw sports facilities as a means of letting space to tenants, so housing developers saw the inclusion of leisure facilities as a means of attracting buyers for their houses. The difficulty for most housing developers came not in raising the capital to build the facilities, but finding some way of funding their continued operation and refurbishment when completed. There is obviously potential for involving the local authority in making these new facilities available to other people living in the area, but few schemes of this nature seem to have been completed.

Summary

There is a synergy and some demand for sport and leisure facilities in the following areas:

Shopping centres   –   More likely for comparison rather than for a specific purpose

In town   –   Sport and leisure facilities should be in-town, but considerable work may be required from the local authority to find the right size of site for the right price

Out-of-town   –   Edge-of-town and out-of-town facilities are common and popular with commercial leisure operators

Offices   –   Health clubs go particularly well in office developments

Housing   –   Community sports and leisure facilities desirable

A definition of partnerships

So, we have identified who the potential partners are and in part where they are interested in developing, assessing the potential for sport and leisure to complement other types of development. The next task is to define the type of partnerships which we will be considering as case studies in the chapters 6, 7 and 8. In broad terms, these partnerships will be assessed under the following headings:

● Partnership arrangements designed to provide new, or to refurbish existing sports facilities through the injection of a capital investment.

● Partnership arrangements for the management of local authority facilities under arranged contracts or CCT. These contracts can offer assistance with revenue funding and some capital investment in return for varied or longer contracts.

● Partnerships which concentrate on revenue support — local sponsorship, marketing of facilities, GP Referral schemes and partnerships which fund sport development and training.

6

Examples of partnerships which can assist with capital funding to refurbish or build sports facilities

This chapter is dedicated to a series of case studies which illustrate successful and in some cases unsuccessful partnerships, designed to provide new or to refurbish existing sports facilities through the injection of a capital investment. In all these cases funding has been provided either through planning gain, or raised by a capital receipt, which the local authority then chose to use for investment in their own sports facilities. There is also a short section on commercial leisure developments which enhance the range of sport and leisure facilities available in any one area. Following each example key issues which contributed to the success or otherwise of the project are highlighted.

Capital receipts
Colchester Leisure Centre

In the late 1980s, Colchester Borough Council decided to redevelop their existing 1960s sports centre, situated on an edge-of-town site at Colchester. The existing sports centre contained a 33 metre swimming pool, sports hall, small multi-purpose hall, squash courts and bar. To create a modern facility, the existing centre was upgraded. The swimming pool had a movable boom installed to create a 25 metre national short course competition pool and additional seating was added. The bar was refurbished and a new juice bar with small health suite added. The increase in revenue earning areas in the existing pool hall maximised income potential. Adjacent to the existing pool, a new split level 500 sq metre leisure pool was built. A new multi-purpose hall was designed to accommodate all indoor sports, but it could also be used for arts and entertainment functions. Bleacher seating will take over 400 spectators and additional free-standing floor seating could increase the audience capacity to 1200. Outside, a multi-purpose all weather pitch was designed for five-a-side football or outdoor hockey. A separate sauna world provided both active and passive facilities with saunas, steam rooms, hydro-massage pools, solaria, treatment room and relaxation area.

The architects, Sargent & Potiriadis, altered the orientation of the centre, so that a new entrance was created off the main road (the old A12).

Partnership funding came from the sale by the local authority of two sites to First Leisure Corporation for ten-pin bowling and McDonalds for a drive-through restaurant. This raised a capital receipt of approximately £1.2 million to be invested in the non-commercial sport and leisure facilities.

Key points

- The new mix of facilities offered at Colchester match changes in customer expectation and use. The new centre offers facilities for all age groups — conventional swimming, leisure swimming, relaxation in the sauna world, indoor and outdoor sports, the ability to host arts and cultural functions. By placing commercial leisure facilities on the

32

site, the mix of facilities available was expanded still further.

- Indoor sports halls can be dominated by five-a-side-football, which excludes much use by other groups for different sports. The provision of an outdoor, all weather pitch, means that most of the five-a-side use can go outside.

- The Colchester sports centre was located on a major arterial road - the old A12, Cowdray Avenue. This made it attractive to private sector commercial leisure owner-operators.

- The total capital receipt raised from the sale of land to McDonalds and First Leisure was available for use by the Council, since the land was sold to the private sector operators before the introduction of the Local Government and Housing Act and the 50% Rule.

- Although the local authority and private sector facilities are situated side by side, there is very little joint marketing of their facilities.

The Guildford Spectrum

The new Guildford Spectrum centre opened in 1993 at a cost close to £30 million. The centre contains a 25 metre, 8 lane swimming pool and a leisure pool, an international size ice rink, 2 court sports hall and health and fitness club. Outside there is an 8 lane running track and also included is a 32 lane, ten-pin bowling centre.

Key points

- The funding for this scheme came from a mix of capital receipts. The largest part came from the sale of an existing athletics track to Tesco for a superstore. Although this capital receipt was received after the introduction of the 50% Rule (Local Government Housing Act), 100 per cent of the receipt was available for the replacement of the athletics track on a different site under the 'Like with Like' regulations. In other words, if the sale of the site to Tesco raised say £25 million, then the local authority could only spend 50 per cent of the capital receipt. However, they could use 100 per cent to pay for the cost of replacing the existing athletics track on another site. So if the new athletics track cost £2 million, they could use £2 million of the £25 million and then only 50 per cent of the remaining £23 million.

- The replacement of 'like with like' facilities on the same site, or on a different site are detailed under the 'in and out' arrangement allowed under regulation 18 of The Capital Finance Regulations outlined in DoE Circular 11/90. This allows local authorities to use 100 per cent of capital receipts when replacing an existing sports facility on the same or another site.

- Now that the Spectrum is open, the Council may in due course sell their existing Guildford Leisure Centre, which is located close to the town centre on a valuable site. Again, they will be able to use the full 100 per cent capital receipt gained from the sale of this site to pay for the Spectrum.

- Guildford Borough Council was one of the first councils in the UK to include ten-pin bowling in a council-owned sport and leisure centre. They hope that the inclusion of this commercial facility will make a revenue surplus, which can be set against the anticipated losses of the more non-commercial swimming facilities and ice rink.

- This project was led from start to finish by Brendan Hanvey, the Director of Technical Services at Guildford Borough Council, who is also in overall charge of planning, architecture and engineering. The Chief Executive is also a sports enthusiast. This leadership and co-ordination of the project was of great importance to the success of the scheme, particularly since there were various vocal and well organised opposition groups to the new development.

- This project was let on a design and build basis after a competition won by Miller Associates with Sunley Leisure. Sadly, Stuart Miller died just a month before the centre was finished.

Cambridge, Parkside

Cambridge Parkside currently comprises an existing 110 feet pool built in 1963, which would cost £1.93 million plus fees to bring up to modern standards. The pool is adjacent to a sports centre, which is owned by the City Council and run as a community trust. The sports centre has the capacity for 10 badminton courts, squash, fitness, catering and a climbing wall. A requirement of the development brief is that the re-development of the swimming pool should link the sports centre with a new swimming pool.

A developer was chosen for Cambridge Parkside by Cambridge City Council in 1985, but the scheme was called in by the DoE and the project eventually stopped in 1989. In 1991, a new scheme comprising £21 million of commercial leisure (24 lane ten-pin bowl, 6 screen multiplex cinema, nightclub, foyer bar, foodcourt and two hotels with a total of 205 beds) was drawn up. It was envisaged that this development would pay for a £5-6 million swimming pool. However, this scheme was stopped by mutual agreement after discouraging observations by various key consultees, including The Royal Fine Arts Commission, who indicated that the scheme was overdeveloping this sensitive site. In May 1993, an additional document, the 'Client Specification', was prepared to clarify the Council's precise requirements for its new facilities and an agreement was then signed with Stock Harvard Developments in July 1993 for a reduced scheme, comprising a new swimming complex, funded by a 160 bed hotel and a 21,000 sq ft nightclub.

Key points

- A very sensitive site, opposite Parker's Piece (open space) and next to Fenners cricket ground. Not only is the local authority worried about the architectural design, but also about over development. Both the Royal Fine Arts Commission, and the Historic Buildings Panel have been involved in the consultation. In order to meet the objections of the Royal Fine Arts Commission a consultant architect was appointed from a list recommended by the Commission, to work on the exterior aspects of the design. The original architects, S & P Ltd, remain responsible for the interior.

- Cambridge learned the lesson of having a site with potential for a £21 million private sector development, but finding that the historic and sensitive nature of the site meant that all of this potential could not be realised. Obviously the current commercial scheme will raise much reduced premiums to be put into a new swimming complex.

- One of the problems of the 1991 scheme was that the leisure brief acknowledging the potential of the site was very different from the planning brief which highlighted the planning restrictions. This highlights the need for both Departments to agree on the scope of the development before any brief is issued.

- The Council has successfully applied to the Department of Environment for extensions of the CCT timetable twice, to gain exemption from putting the existing Cambridge Parkside pool out to CCT, while its future is decided.

- The existing pool was requiring deficit funding each year of just under £400,000. The new pool will include a 25 metre, 8 lane competition pool and a combined diving and teaching pool with movable floor. In addition there will be two flumes and a children's area, a health suite and two cafés. The new pool will be linked through a shared reception with the sports centre.

- In looking for a re-development of Parkside, Cambridge City Council set out with two cardinal principles in their minds. The first was to provide a new pool at no capital cost to the Council. The second was that the running cost must be dramatically lower than the running costs for the existing pool.

- In determining the specification for the new pool and the water area, the Council based its requirements on the outcome of applying the Sports Council's Facilities Planning Model[1], when drawing up its 1993-96 Leisure Strategy.

- The Council will be able to spend 100 per cent of the capital receipt gained from the sale of land for commercial leisure, as it is replacing an existing pool. The rules for the replacement of 'like with like' facilities given under the Guildford Spectrum, apply.

The Norwich Sport Village

It would seem that the Swiss were a few years ahead of the UK in developing partnerships between their public and private sectors. Interhaus Sport, set up by a builder and engineer, began working in Switzerland 15-20 years ago. In the UK its first and to date only project was the Norwich Sport Village, situated on the edge of the City within the remit of Broadland District Council.

The original site was owned by the Gurney Trust and given to the local authority with the proviso that part of the site be used for a sports development. Broadland District Council sold part of the site to Asda for a superstore and used the capital receipt for a partnership with Interhaus for the Norwich Sport Village.

Phase 1, which involved building seven indoor tennis courts and five outdoor ones, five-a-side football pitch, both indoor and outdoor, health club and six squash courts, with a 55 bedroom hotel was paid for by the Council contributing the land and £1 million and Interhaus Sport contributing £6.5 million. Phase 1 opened in 1988. 800 people per week use the gym and 38 classes of aerobics attract 900 users a week.

Phase 2 was a 25 metre, six lane pool with separate leisure pool and two flumes which was opened in 1991. The total contract cost of £4.5 million included a contribution from the local authority of £2.8 million. The completed pool was then sold to the local authority and leased back to the Norwich Sport Village. In 1992 the pool attracted 400,000 visits.

Unlike most private sector-operated tennis facilities, the Sport Village is operated on a pay and play basis. At peak times (Mon-Fri, 6-10pm), the cost of hiring an indoor tennis court for 55 minutes is £17, but there are opportunities for block–booking and a range of off–peak deals available. Ladies' mornings include court hire at £5.50 an hour.

Key points

- The Sport Village finds tennis harder to sell than badminton. They believe that this is due to the predominantly middle class potential of tennis whereas badminton has an additional social dimension. They feel that they are not helped by the Lawn Tennis Association, who part–funded an ITI centre on the other side of Norwich. The LTA contend that they could not have the usage they required at the Sport Village at the right cost.

- The inclusion of a hotel was vital to the tourism potential of Norwich. Since the Sport Village opened, the hotel has increased its occupancy levels, but the rack-rate (average achievable booking fee) per room has decreased. Tourism has extended the season — the British Chess Championships were held at the Village with an attendance of 2,000 people for a week. The Village works with their local TEC, Chamber of Commerce and the local authority. The Norwich Sport Village is very well signposted from whichever direction it is approached and the local authority has ensured the co-operation of local bus companies.

- The people of Norfolk spend only half the national average of income spent on sport and leisure activities.

- The Village is justifiably proud of the service it offers and its staff can take levels 1-3, City and Guilds NVQs in Sport and Hospitality.

- The Sport Village is run as a private limited company. The local authority retain their interest in the centre through one Councillor director. There is no requirement for any revenue support from the Council for the Sports Village. The Sports Village is very involved in the local community and sponsors events like the Broadland Games.

The Vale of White Horse

The Vale of White Horse District Council, which covers an area in the triangle between Newbury, Oxford and Swindon with a population of just over 200,000, was given land for a sports park by a farmer 7 or 8 years ago. The site which lies within the Oxford green belt was to be used for recreation. The local authority sold land elsewhere in the District to Waitrose and are using £2 million of their capital receipt to develop an 8 lane athletics track with a spectator area for 500, two natural sports pitches and two all-weather football pitches. There will also be a changing pavilion.

The remaining six or seven acres have been identified for a private leisure development to provide indoor facilities on a long lease.

Key points

- It is unlikely that a major commercial leisure owner-operator will be interested in taking the opportunity to develop a privately–owned sports centre. The potential is not great enough for commercial leisure and the scheme is more oriented towards non-commercial sport.

- From the interest received by the Council to date, it seems more likely that this opportunity will be taken up by a smaller company, who is either interested in partnerships for sport like Interhaus or the Kettering Leisure Village, or is a CCT contractor. Interested parties have suggested that they might not only provide some capital funding for a privately run indoor scheme, but they also see the potential for taking over the entire development and managing part of it on behalf of the local authority.

- Another alternative solution for the Council is to set up a minority holding company (details of which are given in chapter 7 under the example at Cherwell District Council, page 66).

Royal Quays

The Tyne and Wear Development Corporation was established by Central Government in 1987, with an anticipated lifespan of approximately ten years. Its purpose is to bring about the regeneration of 6,000 acres of land alongside 27 miles of the River Tyne and the River Wear in the North East of England. The land lies within the area of four local authorities — the Cities of Newcastle and Sunderland and the Metropolitan Boroughs of North Tyneside and South Tyneside. The Corporation receives an annual budget from the Department of the Environment and can supplement this with income raised locally — for example by land sales, in addition to funding from the EU. The Corporation's total budget for 1993-1994 is around £50 million. The Corporation's policies are determined by a Board of 13 members, appointed by the Secretary of State for the Environment and drawn from the world of business and industry, local authorities, educational bodies, leisure organisations and the trade unions.

TWDC is involved in around 30 development projects, including six major schemes — Newcastle Business Park, Newcastle Quayside, Royal Quays, Sunderland Enterprise Park, St Peter's Riverside and Viking Industrial Park.

The Royal Quays development at North Shields is the Tyne and Wear Development Corporation's biggest single project, covering 200 acres of land on the north bank of the Tyne. The aim is to bring new homes, jobs and leisure facilities to the site, uplifting the economy and environment of an area far wider than Royal Quays itself. For many years, much of the land stood derelict. But the spectacular setting of the site, forming a giant amphitheatre around the historic Albert Edward Dock, is now being given a totally new lease of life.

TWDC is managing the project and individual schemes within the overall master plan are being carried out by a number of different companies. In all, it has been estimated that by the time it is complete, the total cost of the Royal Quays Project will be around £245 million. Of this, some £84 million will be provided by the Development Corporation.

The first phase of the development comprises 9,000 sq metres of industrial space which includes the Twinings tea packing plant, 500 homes and a 4,000 sq metre water park. A new 12-acre public park called Chirton Dene is being created by the Development Corporation. Around 50,000 trees and shrubs will be planted to landscape the park, which will become the 'green heart' of Royal Quays. Future leisure developments plans may include a 150 bed hotel, ten-pin bowling, multiplex cinema, restaurants and an extension of the nearby preserved steam railway onto the Royal Quays site.

The indoor water park sits at the gateway to the whole site. It cost £8 million and opened in July 1993. There are eight rides, a white knuckle ride and a twister ride, a tube ride and five flumes. A lazy river which runs round the perimeter of the building is used by bathers in tyres. There are waterfalls, water jets, indoor and outdoor water, a wave cannon and cafe terrace. The water park is called Wet 'n' Wild and is operated by Tyneside Waterpark Ltd. 165,000 visitors came within the first six months. Concessionary entry charges are available to residents from surrounding areas.

Key points

- This project demonstrates the ability of Urban Development Corporations to act as enablers for sport and leisure projects.

- TWDC made a substantial contribution towards the capital costs of the waterpark, but are not involved in any revenue subsidy.

- Tyneside Waterpark Ltd signed a code of conduct and worked with the local TEC to ensure that over 50 per cent of the 70 people employed are from the local area.

- The Development Corporation has ensured that concessionary prices are available for the local community.

Lee Valley Regional Park

Lee Valley Regional Park was set up by an act of Parliament in January 1967. It is a Body Corporate Under Seal, but its borrowing powers are set by Central Government and it is subject to controls such as the 50% rule in a similar way to a local authority.

The Regional Park is set along 23 miles from Bromley by Bow to Ware in Hertfordshire and covers 10,000 acres. Its objective is to reclaim land for public leisure and so far it has reclaimed about 3,000 acres. Some of the remaining land is owned by public utilities like the Water companies, some is occupied by farms or gravel pits and some is owned by local authorities. It includes, for example, 300 acres of Hackney Marshes which holds over 100 football pitches. This area used to be owned by the Greater London Council (GLC) and upon its demise, ownership has passed to The London Borough of Hackney.

The Regional Park owns two major sports centres, an Ice Rink and a Leisure Pool, as well as many smaller facilities. Over the past five years it has endeavoured to enter into partnerships with the private sector. So far, two partnership arrangements worthy of note have come to fruition.

The first is at Pickett's Lock, adjacent to the Lee Valley Leisure centre. The leisure centre has a hall with a capacity for 2,000 people, sports hall to take 10 badminton courts, indoor bowls hall, small leisure pool, 8 squash courts, rifle range, snooker, fitness and health suite and catering. Outside there is a 18 hole golf course, golf driving range, one full size all-weather grass pitch and four smaller ones.

The Park Authority is prevented by its statute from selling off land, unless it has no further use for leisure, so rather than selling a site for a multiplex cinema and taking a capital receipt, a site has been leased to UCI for a 12 screen multiplex cinema. The lease is for 125 years and offers the Lee Valley Regional Park an annual rent. The cinema opened in March 1994.

On a nearby part of the site, the Park Authority has chosen a developer who is developing two stand-alone licensed restaurants which will be pre-let to operators.

The second partnership concerns the catering contract for all the catering within the Park's control. The Regional Park is not allowed through its statute to operate its own catering. Instead, it has let a five year contract to National Leisure Catering (NLC) for all its facilities. The partnership offers the Park a profit share and involves NLC investing some capital into improving facilities.

Key points:

- An annual rental, rather than a capital receipt can be more useful to local authority who may wish to avoid engaging the 50% rule or any other Government imposed capital restrictions. It is likely that the sum received from a lease will be less than that received as a lump sum, as most owner-operators prefer to own what they operate, rather than leasing a site. It does however bring in a steady income for the local authority which can be classed as revenue rather than capital. Operators do lease, however, and in the case of Lee Valley, this was the only option.

- Lee Valley Regional Park is a partner with the London Boroughs of Enfield, Hackney, Haringey, Newham, Tower Hamlets and Waltham Forest with the London Planning Advisory Committee and the Department of the Environment in promoting a new initiative, the Lee

Valley Partnership, to regenerate the Lee Valley, described as London's premier manufacturing corridor. The area has Assisted Area Status, awarded by the Government in 1993 and in 1994, the Lee Valley has been designated an European Regional Development Fund — 'Objective Two' area. It is the only part of London eligible for this funding from the European Community.

- The catering contract has nothing to do with CCT, but in some ways the mechanism is similar and the arranged contract brings benefits both to the Park and the contractor. The Park has a five year contract and an injection of capital which will not come under the scrutiny of their capital controls.

Kettering Leisure Village

The Kettering Leisure Village is a unique project. It is a regional centre for sport, leisure and entertainment, built in a rural area of Northamptonshire with capital injected by way of a capital receipt from the local authority and with substantial funding from a private sector company.

In 1987, Kettering Borough Council carried out a review of their leisure strategy with the help of consultants. Kettering itself has a population of around 45,000 and the Borough 80,000. The total population of Northamptonshire is 600,000.

The local authority had a small 25 metre swimming pool in the centre of the town, a converted drill hall and conventional sports hall in nearby Desborough. At the time there was much talk about the Wonderworld project in nearby Corby (population 55,000), but perhaps more importantly the prospect of the A14, A1-M1 link which would be built on the edge of town.

The leisure strategy identified two sites for a new leisure centre and the local authority decided that it needed to approach the private sector for assistance if a project of any size or significance was to be realised.

After some deliberation a site on the edge of town, which was owned by the Duke of Buccleuch and used for agricultural purposes, was identified as the best site. It offered 110 acres of net developable land which would be mainly used for housing. The town also required a new drainage system and the site was also identified as an ideal place for a new reservoir.

Although the site was not owned by the Borough Council, they did own a recreation ground which would be needed to provide a new access if the full potential of the site was to be realised. A legal precedent set by the Stokes v Cambridge case established that if a site was needed for access, then the owner of that site was entitled to a share, often around a third of the value of developable land, as compensation. In Kettering, the recreation ground owned by the Borough Council, if used for a new access, would open up an additional sixty acres for development. It followed that a third of this site, i.e. 20 acres, would be due to the Borough Council in compensation. In due course these 20 acres were valued at £6 million which became the basis of the Council's contribution to the capital cost of the leisure centre.

Between September and November 1988 a public consultation exercise established what sort of leisure facilities were on the shopping list for a new sport and leisure facility. This exercise was followed by an invitation for the private sector to tender as potential partners in the scheme. Approaches were received from Redelco/Alfred McAlpine, Penhale, Northwest Holst, Sunley Projects and Conder. Redelco/Alfred McAlpine and Norwest Holst were shortlisted and Redelco/Alfred McAlpine chosen.

Negotiations with the landowner established that 20 acres would given for a leisure complex (in addition to the 20 acres offered as compensation for the access land). Alfred McAlpine priced the capital cost of the overall project at £15 million of which £6 million would be provided by the Borough Council and £9 million provided by Redelco.

There then came the introduction of the 1989 Local Government and Housing Act, which imposed the 50% rule. The Council was aware that this would limit their contribution to £3 million — 50 per cent of the £6 million (in retrospect this could have been reduced to £1.5 million if it was deemed that the land had been sold for a housing development — in this case only 25 per cent of the capital receipt could be used for Council's own purposes - the rest had to be used to redeem debt). The Council therefore decided that the only way to circumvent the 50% rule was to set up the project through a third party and use nominees.

During 1990 the Council became increasingly frustrated at the lack of progress on the sale of the 20 acres for housing or on the leisure project and felt powerless, from their arms' length perspective, to do anything about it. At the same time the UK entered recession and land prices fell. The Council realised that the project was floundering and therefore decided to enter into a Section 106 Planning Agreement so that instead of accepting £6 million in cash for the land due them in compensation for providing access, they would accept the 20 acres and attempt to sell this land for housing themselves.

The Council negotiated the sale of the housing site to Wilcon Homes for £3.7 million. Redelco struck up a deal with East Midlands Electricity through their subsidiary Lincoln Green Energy, who were interested in introducing a revolutionary heat exchange system to the leisure complex. In time Lincoln Green took a 25 per cent share in Redelco and a 20 per cent equity share in the newly formed company, Kettering Leisure Village Limited (KLVL).

By this time, it became apparent that the £15 million initially required for the project had shrunk. The centre was therefore redesigned, and in particular an innovative form of roofing replaced by a more conventional structure. The local authority realised that it would need to fund independently the 8 lane all-weather running track and outdoor multipurpose track. The local authority then tried to relet the contract for the building of the leisure complex, asking contractors to submit a fixed price of £10.4 million which would include an equity injection of £1 million. Following the interview of a number of contractors, J E Elliott were chosen, but they almost immediately went into liquidation.

The £10.4 million and additional enabling works was split between the Council and KLVL. The Council contributed £3.5 million and KLVL £8 million. Balfour Beatty were chosen as the contractor and the Kettering Leisure Village opened in July 1993.

The Leisure Village can roughly be divided into two. The whole site which it occupies (20 acres) is let from the landowner to the Borough Council on a 125 year lease. This is then sublet to Kettering Leisure Village, who then sublet back to the Council their half of the centre. The local authorities capital contribution funded a 2,000 seated entertainment hall which can hold 12 badminton courts and a 4 badminton court ancillary hall. They paid for the County gymnastics training centre, dance studio, crèche, public meeting room and a three–court tennis hall. The tennis hall was partly funded from £100,000 made available from the LTA, Sports Council, and All England Lawn Tennis Club through the Indoor Tennis Initiative. The gymnastics pit was part funded by the East Midland Region of the Sports Council.

KLVL paid for the capital costs of the leisure pool and leisure ice rink, 9-pin bowling, Quasar centre, snooker club, catering, health suite and wine bar. Redelco manage the entire complex and have a 15 year management agreement to cover the part of the Village which was paid for by the local authority.

Key points:

- The project took five years to come to fruition. The complicated nature of the land transaction caused initial delays and the anticipated effects of the 50% rule, along with falling land prices created a major headache. In the end, the relaxation of the 50% rule between November 1992 and December 1993 meant that the Borough Council could use its entire capital receipt for the development of this centre.

- The scale of the complex could not be justified for its immediate population of 80,000 residents in the Borough. However, it is seen as an regional centre by the Borough Council and KLVL, taking advantage of the excellent location of the new A1/M1 link road and making the facility accessible to the 5.6 million residents within a catchment area of 50 minutes drive time.

- All the potential partners came from the construction industry, except Redelco who are really a management company interested in providing capital investment. It would seem, therefore, that none of the large owner-operators considered that the site was suitable for stand-alone commercial leisure. The Borough Council insisted on the provision of municipal facilities as part of the overall design which precluded the option of a stand-alone commercial leisure operation.

- At first sight the mix seems very sports–oriented and totally uncommercial. However, the multi-purpose hall is ideal for pop concerts and its standing capacity of 3,000 is greater than anything else between the NEC in Birmingham, the Cambridge Corn Exchange, the De Montfort Hall in Leicester and the Northampton theatre.

- KLVL and their general manager Malcolm Murphy really do appreciate the argument of critical mass and the need of the Leisure Village to attract all age groups and markets for repeat visits.

- Project management and equity involvement from Lincoln Green Energy ensured that the project was completed at 4 per cent over budget. This compared very favourably with overspends on more conventional projects such as Ponds Forge in Sheffield or the Plymouth Pavilions.

- Flexibility for future change has also been essential for KLVL. The initial idea for incorporating an indoor golf range was abandoned and was replaced by an agreement for a Family Fun Centre. The partnership with the Borough Council has also ensured that many of the normal irritations for commercial leisure operators such as licensing, safety and environmental health have never become problems. Once they had entered into the partnership, the Borough Council did their best to ensure that KLVL were given every assistance with the set-up and on-going operation of the Leisure Village.

- KLVL have started slowly, determined to ensure that their product is right. Initially they concentrated on attracting the 78,000 population of the Borough to use the facility and in six months they have achieved a throughput of 500,000. In the beginning they had some difficulty in changing customer usage patterns that previously were accustomed to making a visit to a sports/leisure centre for one purpose only. It took time to establish usage of one facility, the habit of having a meal and relaxing, followed by use of another facility. The task has been one of linking use of facilities in the mind of visitor and user through packaging and pricing initiatives.

- Working with community groups and the Police, KLVL have sought to encourage off-peak usage by the unemployed, senior citizens, students and those on income support. They realise that the centre costs are generally fixed, therefore the encouragement of off-peak use creates a contribution towards the operation and assist in providing a true community facility, with which individuals and groups alike can identify.

- KLVL have established a local bus service partly sponsored by the County and Borough Councils, United Counties, who operate the service and a local hotel. In spite of the contributions the project was costing the Leisure Village £12,000 a year, but the buses have now been re-routed so that the Leisure Village is not necessarily seen as a destination, but as a stop on a route which takes in local housing estates, the hospital and the town centre. On one night each week, a bus calls at the five local schools in turn and offers free trips to the leisure centre to children as they go home between 3-4 pm.

- Sponsorship has been a key revenue earner for KLVL. Weetabix, a family–owned company whose factory and headquarters are on the edge of Kettering, sponsor the indoor tennis centre. Their name can be clearly seen from the A1/M1 link, just as their factory is a landmark on the Inter-City train journey to Kettering. Pepsi sponsor the ice rink, having the naming rights to 'Pepsi Crystal World'. This sponsorship involvement enables the company to have a high profile with its target youth market who are the core group using this facility. Success in this area breeds success. Recent contracts have been entered into with Allied Dunbar for a health suite, the Temperance Society are associated with a youth access control scheme and a local radio station and seat supplier have their company represented on the reverse of all concerts tickets.

- The local authority were keen that the Leisure Village did not operate a membership scheme. Instead it has an Associate Scheme. Initially, the concept offered by Kettering Leisure Village for owners of associate cards to use the facility were too complicated for the local people. The system was subsequently simplified in terms of benefits available, i.e. discounts and ability to book facilities by telephone, and this is now proving successful.

- The Leisure Village has not escaped competition from other operators. An independent operator has opened a purpose built nightclub in the town centre. The Leisure Village has responded by offering £1 a pint beer nights (its purchasing power enabling its beer prices to be kept low). They have identified niche markets, namely Jazz and Comedy nights and have a permanent 2 am licence in the Village Club which hosts these events.

- The Leisure Village is a remarkable project which may become a landmark for future partnership schemes. Only time will tell, however, if KLVL can repay a debt burden of £7 million and make an operating profit.

The Indoor Tennis Initiative[2]

In 1986, The Lawn Tennis Association (LTA), The All England Lawn Tennis Club and The Sports Council agreed a five year programme to build indoor tennis centre which would run on a 'pay-as-you-play' basis. This was followed by the launch in 1992 of a five year Facility Plan, which aims to provide £63 million of capital funding for tennis facilities.

In proposing this strategy, the LTA sought not only to improve tournament venues and training facilities for elite tennis players, but also to encourage grass-roots participation in tennis.

When the five to seven year Plan was launched, Britain did not have a single clay court tournament venue — a surface on which 40 per cent of international events are staged, and only two acrylic court venues existed to host major international events. The LTA acknowledged that investment in first class facilities was therefore essential if the UK is to compete internationally in attracting players, sponsors and spectators. Alongside these tournament venues, 25 training centres with both indoor and outdoor courts were to be developed to assist counties to improve playing standards.

Until this time, many clubs had benefited from the LTA Loans Scheme, but few had been able to undertake indoor court projects. Only 3 per cent of voluntary members clubs had indoor clubs. The target was to stimulate a further 40 clubs to build 80 indoor courts.

Leaving aside tournament venues, county centres and training facilities, ITI grants for building new facilities to encourage participation are in the main given to a local authority. The local authority enters into a 'partnership' agreement with the ITI for 21 years. The facilities have to be built on local authority-owned land with a minimum of 4-6 indoor and 4-6 outdoor courts. The facilities have to be built in accordance with an ITI performance specification and be used solely for tennis, although other sports and social elements can be added to each scheme. An ITI centre cannot be operated on a 'membership' basis and the maximum charges for courts have to be agreed with the LTA. During 1994, ITI centres can only charge a maximum of £13 per hour for a court. Many centre operate below this limit and offer other special rates for juniors, depending on where they are in the country.

The first ITI centre was opened in St Albans in 1988. By the end of phase one, an investment of £25 million had created 24 new centres and 107 indoor courts. Phase two concentrated on specific targets of inner cities and large conurbations and only proposals in these areas are considered for a grant. By the end of 1994 there will be 33 centres operating throughout the UK.

ITI Centres exist in the following locations:

Wigan	St Albans	Warrington
Welwyn Garden City	Bodmin	Wigan
Sunderland	Solihull	Nottingham
Islington	Deal	Cambridge
Sheffield	Sutton	Stirling
Swindon	Corby	Newcastle-Upon-Tyne
Gosforth	Hove	Brighton
Swansea	Bournemouth	Portsmouth
Wrexham	Kettering	Arfon
Liverpool	Wirral	

Under Construction:

Glasgow	North Kensington	Birmingham
South Ribble	Edinburgh	Aberdeen
Taunton		

Key points:

- Partners for ITI centres vary, but the recipients of grants are in the main the local authority. Taylor Woodrow part funded the Swindon scheme, in the Wirral the project was part of a City Challenge bid.

- In Wales, the ITI initiative part funded a North Wales Regional Tennis Centre. Additional funding came from the Garden Village Tennis Club, The Sports Council for Wales, the Welsh Tourist Board, The Foundation for Sports and the Arts and Wrexham Maelor Borough Council. The tennis centre was the third most popular indoor tennis centre of the nineteen ITI schemes set up in 1992.

- In Corby, Archer Leisure's subsidiary Centre Court Leisure has become a partner with the District Council. Archer Leisure are working with the LTA on further indoor tennis schemes.

- Future schemes currently under consideration may include a wide range of facilities on sites adjacent to ITI centres. There is no reason why commercial leisure facilities such as ten-pin bowling, cinemas and nightclubs should not provide some funding as a capital receipt.

- It was only in the mid–1980s, when the television rights were renegotiated for Wimbledon, that funding from this tournament became so significant to the development of British Tennis. The LTA have used these funds as a Governing Body of sport so that they can act as an enabler. The funding from the LTA, the All England Lawn Tennis Club and the Sports Council provides pump priming for ITI schemes. It is, however, essential that these funds are matched by funds from the local authority and other private sector partners.

Kinsale Hall Country House Hotel

Kinsale Hall lies within the Borough of Delyn in Clwyd, on the Dee Estuary in North East Wales. The Borough of Delyn has a population of around 65,000 and covers 180 sq miles. The largest town is Flint, with a population of approximately 13,000 inhabitants.

The original company which built Kinsale Hall Country House Hotel went into receivership. In order to create a more viable proposition, the new owners approached the Borough Council with an idea to develop a 9 hole golf course with club house facilities and a golf driving range. The owners needed to convince their bankers that these new facilities would generate a guaranteed income and so entered into a partnership with the local authority.

In essence, the owners of the hotel are building the new golf facilities on land they own. In return for a five year agreement, the local authority are paying a 'rent' for 80 per cent of the use of the golf facilities. All the income from use during their 80 per cent of the time will go to the local authority.

Key points:

- The local authority had no 'pay-as-you-play' golf facilities within the Borough.

- The 'rent' for the 5 year period is fixed and the local authority hope that they will make a profit through the anticipated income.

- In order to track the income from the new facilities, the local authority will install a modem link from the point of sale to a Council owned control point.

- The local authority will determine and control the tariff to be charged for all facilities with the owners of the hotel.

- The hotel owners are guaranteed an income from the 'rent' for the 80 per cent of use by the local authority. In turn, they will be able to offer their guests use of the facilities during the remaining 20 per cent of the time available.

Planning gain

In 1993, The Sports Council published a book which gives 19 case studies of sport and leisure projects achieved through Planning Gain X which should be considered as further reading on this section.

Jarman Fields, Hemel Hempstead

In July 1987 a Dacorum Borough Council Recreation Strategy identified the site of Jarman Fields for a major mixed-use development, which would include sport and leisure without recourse to the rate fund. The site, part of which had at one stage been a refuse tip, was located on the edge of town, covering 50 acres. It contained eight football pitches which would need relocation. Hemel Hempstead has a population of 80,000 with 132,000 in the Borough. Its catchment, however, is excellent. The site at Jarman Fields is situated just five minutes from junction 8 of the M1 and about 10 minutes from the M25. St Albans, Harpenden and Watford are within easy reach.

In September 1987, Ladbroke Group Properties Limited was chosen as the developer of a scheme for a superstore, hotel and major multi-leisure centre. Their partner for the sport and leisure facilities was Rank Leisure, who would operate a six screen cinema, ten-pin bowling, nightclub, bar, laser games, restaurant and fast food diner. Rank would also build and operate a water world, leisure ice rink and indoor bowls. The developer was also required to build an athletics track at Jarman Fields, along with a children's play area, provision of some public open space and the relocation the existing football pitches to a new site and provide the new pitches with changing facilities. In addition, a sum of money was required for the Council to purchase some replacement public open space to replenish that lost through the development.

Key points

- The project marks a first in the history of partnerships in the UK. Not only will Rank Leisure build and operate water world (leisure pool), ice rink and indoor bowls centre, but they will also be responsible for the operation of these facilities at no cost to the Council. The Council has been closely involved in the specification of these facilities, but will not retain the right to influence pricing.

- Some capital funding for the non-commercial sport facilities will come from Ladbroke, arising from the sale of land to the superstore and Hilton hotel. Any revenue support required will be cross-subsided from the commercial leisure facilities operated by Rank.

- The Council already provides conventional swimming facilities and indoor sports facilities at three sites elsewhere in the Borough.

- At the start of the project there was major opposition, not only from the Opposition Party, but also from a very articulate Action Group, who enjoyed support from the local papers. The Council was accused of not carrying out adequate market research in their choice of developer. The opposition was particularly concerned about the introduction of private sector operators for the sport and leisure facilities. The County Council opposed the project on the grounds of increased traffic.

- At the beginning of the project the Council decided, in view of the protracted and specialist nature of the negotiations, to instruct consultant London Solicitors.

- The Council appointed a Management Team comprising of the Council's Directors of Planning and Law and Administration, Chief Engineer and Chief Valuer for the project, led by Mary Pedlow, the Director of Community and Leisure. The strength of Mary Pedlow's leadership along with the support of the seven Council Chief Officers at Decorum has been paramount in ensuring that this project continued. The project team was given as much devolved responsibility from a Project Committee (styled the Jarman Fields Committee) as was possible, leaving major strategic decisions to be taken by the Committee.

- Cultural compatibility has its problems. The culture of a public sector local authority is very different from the culture of a large property developer. The local authority, which has a difficult task to perform in balancing its competing interests as planning authority, leisure provider, land owning public body and as agent for the highway authority, did a magnificent job in this case in achieving a solution satisfactory to the majority. Inevitably this gave rise to a degree of local community friction and distrust of the decision to involve the private sector.

- Looking at the project from the private sector's viewpoint, they feel that considerable weight has been given by the Council to the opposition of a few.

- Changes to the design of the project have been required by the Development Control Committee — for example the need to move the footprint of the building 1.5 m caused some delay. Changes to some aspects of the other elements of the Jarman Fields Scheme have required full approval from the Development Control Committee, rather than approval at Officer level.

The Finchley Pool, Barnet

The London Borough of Barnet sought proposals from the private sector for the development of an indoor/outdoor swimming complex on part of the site of the former Finchley Lido, which had been closed for two years. The valuable site is located on the junction of the North Circular Road in Finchley. The remainder of the site was available for a commercial development and a development brief was issued to interested companies with the proviso that the new pool complex must be funded as a planning gain from any commercial leisure development.

The Council shortlisted two companies from the fourteen proposals received following the placement of a national advertisement, and the scheme submitted by THI Developments was the eventual winner.

THI proposed a 10 screen multiplex cinema, nightclub, 40 lane ten-pin bowling and restaurants. However, the Council's Planning Committee rejected the outline planning application on the grounds that the nightclub was considered inappropriate to the nearby residential area and a revised parking scheme was required.

A revised scheme, which took on board the Council's reservations was quickly submitted and obtained the necessary planning permission.

The pool complex, which will cost around £2.75 million and be operational from summer 1995, will have a conventional 25 metre pool with spectator seating, separate leisure pool, health suite, meeting rooms, cafe and social areas. The area's history of having an outdoor lido for over 70 years will be recreated by the inclusion of outdoor pools with sunbathing and seating areas.

The swimming pools and other leisure developments together with the adjacent David Lloyd Finchley Racquets Centre, an indoor golf centre and indoor bowls adjacent to the site will offer a complete mix of sport and leisure facilities and is expected to attract customers from far afield.

Key points

- The London Borough of Barnet will acquire a new indoor/outdoor swimming pool completed at no capital cost to the Council.

- The Council recognised that the commercial leisure development to be constructed on the remainder of the site must cover the capital cost of the new pool complex. It must also be compatible with other leisure developments operating immediately adjacent to the site.

- As part of the development brief, the Council retained the right to determine the future management of the pool complex.

- The revenue cost for operating the pools will be funded from the Council's existing revenue budget, which includes the costs of operating the previous open air pool and a small nearby pool in Squires Lane, which will be closed when the new complex becomes operational.

- The Council recognised that the commercial leisure operators were unlikely to be interested in operating the community swimming pool. The solution of handing over the facility to the Council once construction was complete for the Council to operate themselves or tender it through the CCT process was considered to be a sensible one.

- Private sector companies who are interested in managing swimming pools are unlikely to be the same companies who are successful at operating commercial leisure facilities.

- The Council commented that public/private sector partnership developments can be successful, providing the development brief is clear and both parties appreciate the constraints and problems in their respective areas. It is most important to the on-going dialogue that mutual respect is maintained throughout the process.

Dulwich Hamlet

Kings College London owned an underused sports ground, Dulwich Hamlet, in an area known as Dog Kennel Hill. The site comprised a sports ground, outdoor football pitch with pavilion changing, tennis courts and a run-down football ground with stands and terraces which was let to Dulwich Hamlet Football Team. In a unique partnership between King's College and J Sainsbury, the site was developed and the sports facilities enhanced and/or replaced on a separate site. The local authority also obtained planning benefits, including an all-weather pitch on land owned by the Council immediately adjoining the west boundary of the new football ground.

The new development comprised a 68,000 sq ft. J Sainsbury's superstore, car parking for nearly 500 cars, a new public open space and a newly constructed football ground, including stand, pitch, and floodlighting on the site of the old ground. The sports facilities for King's College Medical School were replaced on another site in the area.

Key points

- For King's College, London, the objective was to achieve a capital receipt for investment elsewhere within the academic and medical facilities that they own. The sports facilities on the site were still required, but needed investment and were under-used. King's College acted an enabler to engineer a successful solution to the redevelopment of the site to the advantage of all members of the partnership.

- For Sainsburys, the need for the store was justified by a catchment of over 200,000 people and no Sainsbury store built in the area for over ten years.

- For the London Borough of Southwark, as local planning authority, its objective was to secure through a planning agreement benefits for the local community to offset the perceived demerits of the scheme and so enhance the proposed development and ameliorate its impact on the local environment. The three acre public open space, whose upkeep is the joint responsibility of King's and Sainsburys and the all-weather pitch were two significant aspects of the planning agreement. Others included funding of ecological schemes in the immediate area and environmental improvements to an adjoining housing estate.

- 350 new jobs, both full- and part-time, the majority of which are available to local people were provided by the J Sainsbury development.

- Dulwich Hamlets leased a football club which had fallen into disrepair and was in need of updating. The new stadium has 3,000 seats, bar, weight training room and changing area.

Beckenham Place Park

A 200 acre park owned and managed by the London Borough of Lewisham, but located in two Boroughs (Lewisham and Bromley). Existing 18 hole golf course and grade 2 listed property in Woodlands with some football pitches. The property housed the Mander and Mitchenson Theatre Collection which provides a valuable archival resource. The maintenance and management of the park were subject to CCT. There was a demand for increased and improved facilities; the upkeep of the park and its contents were costing the local authority in excess of £100,000 in revenue subsidy each year. The park would require a capital injection of between £2-4 million to bring its current facilities up-to-date, but there were constraints on capital expenditure.

In 1989, Lewisham engaged Touche Ross as consultants to assess the potential for attracting private sector investment into the park, following which Hillier Parker were employed to develop a marketing and planning brief for the site. 200 expressions of interest were received and the Council shortlisted 19 consortia for interview. They chose David Lloyd Leisure, who were prepared to take over management of the park, restore the listed buildings and increase the golf course to 27 holes with a driving range, improve the infrastructure such as access, car parking etc., and build a new David Lloyd Tennis Club.

The site would be leased to David Lloyd for a rent on a 99 year lease. The financial arrangements included capital improvements, annual rent and a share of the turnover of the tennis club and golf courses for the local authority. Although the tennis club would be operated as a private sector facility, there would be guaranteed community use and new under five's club.

Two schemes were submitted for planning submission and both were called in by the Department of the Environment. A decision on the public enquiry is expected in Spring 1994.

In May 1993, David Lloyd took over the management and maintenance of the existing golf course for a minimum of six years on a CCT contract. It was agreed that once planning approval had been received following the Enquiry, the development and management agreement for the whole site was unconditional, and work must start on the tennis centre within three months. If no planning approval agreement was given then David Lloyd was required to give nine months' notice to give up management of the existing golf course.

Key points

- The aim of the local authority was to reduce its revenue spending on the upkeep of the park, to attract external investment for renovation of listed buildings and to achieve new sports facilities for use by the local community.

- The site application was called in by DoE because it occupies a sensitive site on the boundary of the London Borough of Bromley. Well-organised opposition was mounted to the building of a indoor tennis centre on what was previously public open space.

- Many London Boroughs own land designated as public open space, some of which was gained from the dissolution of the Inner London Education Authority (ILEA). They argue that this land is surplus to their needs. Residents who live immediately adjacent to the park suffer from a not uncommon NIMBY (Not In My Backyard) attitude to development on land on which they can walk and exercise their dogs.

- The London Borough of Lewisham is Labour controlled. Not all members were in favour of this development which involved the provision of a privately-operated tennis facility. There was also some trade union opposition to the management and maintenance of Council Services.

- David Lloyd Leisure has already built two indoor tennis centres on green belt and three on public open space. It is therefore difficult for them to understand why this development has been called in by the DoE.

David Lloyd Leisure

David Lloyd retired as a professional tennis player and coach in 1980. During his time as a player, he had played for the British Davis Cup team for ten years and also reached the doubles semi-final at Wimbledon.

In 1980, David Lloyd formed a company to build and run the first commercially successful indoor tennis centre in Britain. In 1993, the company was successfully floated on the London Stock Market. David Lloyd Leisure Plc now owns and operates six tennis and fitness clubs in and around the London area, plus a seventh club in Eastbourne and an eighth in Glasgow.

Key points:

- David Lloyd Clubs are situated in Bushey, Chigwell, Eastbourne, Enfield, Finchley, Hounslow, Raynes Park and Glasgow.

- Seven of the sites occupied by David Lloyd Leisure Clubs have been built on land owned by local authorities. The land has been provided either at a peppercorn rent for 125 years, or on a profit share basis with the local authority or a premium for the lease.

- On average each club has 4,000 members and creates 70 full-time jobs. The cost of membership for the clubs in London includes a joining fee and then monthly payments of between £50 to £75 for individual and family membership.

- Six of the David Lloyd Clubs have community use which is agreed and controlled by the local authority.

- Many of the members of a David Lloyd Club join for the health and fitness facilities — they have never played tennis and learn once they join.

- In Enfield and Chigwell, the rental was dependent on the provision of indoor green bowling for the local community. Members of the club can use this facility free, but there is strong community involvement from the local bowls club who have use on certain days.

Elephant and Castle

The leisure centre at the Elephant and Castle in the London Borough of Southwark was built in the late 1970s. It was one of the first leisure pools to built in the UK. Three phases were originally proposed, of which two have been completed. A leisure pool was complemented by a teaching pool with a two court sports hall. A 25 or 33 metre competition pool was never built.

By the late 1980s the pool structure was in a poor condition. The design of the building meant that it was very difficult to manage. The roof and glazing required complete replacement. The Elephant and Castle leisure centre was losing customers to more modern competing facilities in Lewisham, Greenwich and Brixton.

Amec Urban Development put forward plans for the re-development of the site. The new development would include teaching facilities for the London Institute and accommodation for over 1,300 students. The local authority were asked for a £1 million capital contribution and as a planning gain would be provided with a new facility to include a 25 metre competition pool, a leisure pool, teaching pool, two court sports hall, health suite with dance studio, sauna, solarium and 1,000 sq ft of library space.

There has been substantial (some Councillors would say overwhelming) opposition from local groups and residents. The application has now been called-in by the Secretary of State for his decision following a public inquiry. No date has yet been fixed for the inquiry, but it is not expected to be until June/July at the earliest with a final decision not until late autumn at the earliest.

Key points:

- A classic example of partnership thinking in terms of urban regeneration.

- The partnership involves an educational establishment which makes an ideal tenant for a pre-let of space. This creates a climate for the best type of development where the developer can tie up the use of the space before building begins.

- The Elephant and Castle is a unique site. Not only is it sensitive because of its location, it is also very valuable. Few sites could raise the sort of premium which would allow a leisure development costing over £12 million to be funded with only a capital contribution of £1 million coming from the local authority.

- It now remains to be seen, in the light of the public enquiry, if the scheme will go ahead.

Edinburgh — Leith Waterworld and Drumbrae Swimming Pool

The Leith Waterworld was opened in 1992 and cost £7 million. Funding for the scheme came from the sale of the Leith Central Station site by Edinburgh City Council to the Walker Group. The site had been derelict for some years.

The new development includes a superstore, Scotmid and the refurbishment of some small shops and offices which surround the site. A new Job Centre was created and the PSA took over some of the space for local offices.

Funding for the adjacent leisure pool came through grants from the Scottish Sports Council, the Scottish Development Agency and, as a planning gain, from the Walker Group.

Over a three year period, the City Council has also been in discussions with Balfour Beatty to build a new housing development at Drumbrae. The site was not in the green belt, but was public open space. Through local opposition and a realisation by the authority that the housing would cause over-development of the site, the planning gain has not been realised. However, the City Council will fund a community 25 metre six lane swimming pool, with one and a half court sports hall, fitness suite and crèche. The capital cost is £3 million and it is possible that a library may be added in a second phase.

Key points:

- The Walker Group have been very active in Scotland over recent years in developing mixed-use sites which contain sport and leisure facilities.

- At Leith, the funding from the planning gain must have been subject to the 50% rule, as even if the site was given to the developer for a very small sum, the district auditor would have needed to put a value on the site.

- Once completed, the developer passed the Leith Waterworld over to the City Council who operate the complex and are responsible for its revenue costs.

- The example at Drumbrae shows how good schemes can go awry through localised opposition and planning problems. It is a credit to the City Council that the scheme will still go ahead without assistance from the housing developer.

Towyn and Kinmel Bay

Colwyn Borough Council have entered into an unusual partnership with the owner of a Trotting Track. Trotting is extremely popular in France and Scandinavia and involves horses riding round a 800 metre arena with a jockey seated in a Sulky.

In Towyn, North Wales, a local owner-operator, Billie Williams, approached the Council for planning permission to develop a trotting track with a grandstand on land owned by Colwyn Borough Council. The site is adjacent to a caravan park which provides 60,000 bed spaces in the summer. In adjoining areas, the local authority has developed a country park and factory units.

The local authority agreed to grant a long lease (20 years plus) for the site in return for a peppercorn rent. In return, they asked for the provision of three football pitches, which are situated in the centre of the trotting track, three tennis courts, bowls green, fitness room and associated changing facilities.

As a further development, Colwyn Borough Council have attracted a grant of £40,000 from the Foundation for Sport and the Arts, with an offer of a further £100,000 if they can provide matching funding. This has been achieved with funds from the local authority, the Welsh Sports Council and a contribution from the flood fund left over from the 1990 floods in the area. This funding will be used to construct a one court sports hall.

Key points

- The population of the Borough of Colwyn is only 56,000 with a population out of season of 5,000 in Towyn and Kinmel Bay.

- This imaginative partnership proves the theory of 'make the list of possible partners as wide as possible', particularly if you are situated in a rural area.

- The development of the Trotting Track attracts coverage from Welsh television for its summer meetings and has therefore brought additional investment in this area.

The Branston Golf and Country Club

East Staffordshire Borough Council owned a site in Burton-on-Trent which was leased to Branston Golf Club Limited to operate an 18 hole golf course. In 1990, the company was acquired by Burton Inns. An extended tenancy on the lease from the local authority was negotiated which allowed a small acreage to be sold to Westbury and Barratt for housing, capital was made available to provide a new golf clubhouse incorporating substantial health and fitness facilities.

The 18 hole golf course has been enhanced by the addition of a golf driving range. The golf club currently has a membership of 800. A new clubhouse is currently under construction with a 20,000 sq ft health and fitness club. The club will have a 17 metre swimming pool, sauna, steam room, 2,000 sq ft gym and aerobics studio, together with a bar, restaurant and meeting rooms, as well as 1,000 sq ft of retail for a small shop.

It is envisaged that the health and fitness club will attract an additional 1,200 members. It will be opened in September 1994.

Key points:

- In return for granting the long lease to the Branston Golf Club Limited, East Staffordshire Borough Council have taken a 19 per cent share in a new company.

- The new company will pay the local authority a commercial rent for the site and share profits from the new facilities.

- Part of the agreement requires the golf course to be open to the local community on a pay as you play basis.

- The new health club will be run on a membership basis.

Commercial leisure developments

There are some leisure developments that do not involve the public sector at all in the funding, although obviously the local authority will still be required to grant planning permission. It is worth highlighting several of these commercial leisure schemes which have been successful, as if the appropriate site is available they may be worth encouraging as a means of attracting a wide greater range of leisure facilities in any one area.

The Wirral

Unilever owned the freehold of a site in the Wirral, adjacent to a retail park. Anchor tenants included Asda, McDonalds, Texas, Children's World, Halfords and other edge-of-town retailers. THI Developments acquired a plot of around 15 acres for a leisure development and obtained outline planning permission.

The attraction of this site for Rank Leisure lay in its accessibility from the A41 and a one-way system round the site which would draw all visitors to the retail area past the site for the leisure. It was therefore agreed that THI would develop the site, shell and car parking to Rank's design and specification, which would then be sold to Rank for fitting out. Once the shell was sold to Rank Leisure, then Rank took over the long lease and have a leasehold agreement direct with Unilever.

The shell of the building covers approximately 91,000 sq ft and inside the mall is designed to represent a typical New York Street. The walls are weathered stone and brick and the floor looks like a street with paving stones and proper sidewalks. There are painted shop fronts and murals, a barber's shop, free standing vending, fire hydrants and next to a sign that says "Don't even think of parking here" is a yellow New York taxi cab sponsored by a local taxi firm! US mail boxes act as litter bins and a dark blue 'sky' ceiling sets off the street lighting and illuminated advertising signs.

Facilities include a seven screen Odeon Cinema, Top Rank twenty-four lane multi-bowl, disco for 18-25 year olds and a nightclub for the over 25s, a fun bar themed with American memorabilia, amusements and a fast food restaurant.

Key points:

- From start to finish, the timescale from assessment of the site to opening the facilities took under two years. Without any requirement for planning gain or the provision of non-commercial sports facilities, Rank Leisure were able to complete the project in as short a time as possible.

- The Planning Department of the Wirral MBC worked hard in partnership with THI and Rank to ensure a clear path for the development

- The local authority were particularly happy with the all-weather, enclosed leisure facilities. The open mall and single entrance was attractive and secure.

Huddersfield

An in-town/edge of town centre site owned by Kirklees Metropolitan Borough Council, but leased to a Mill. To be re-developed by developers Tolent McGivern. Rank Leisure plan to occupy the 4.5 acre site with a 87,000 sq ft multi-leisure scheme for ten-pin bowling, bingo and two nightclubs.

Key points:

- Kirklees MBC have been enormously supportive of the private sector leisure development. Any planning problems have been instantly dealt with to ease the passage of the scheme.

- An in-town site, but with land that is cheap enough to allow for a leisure development. The cost of building will also be reasonable in this part of the country.

- The M62 is only three miles away and a catchment of 345,000 live within 7 miles or 15 minutes drive time. This makes the location additionally attractive.

The Mansion House, Reading

A local businessman, Benjamin Childs, built the Mansion House in 1760 for his wife. The house was extensively rebuilt in the 1800s by the architect James Wright Sanderson for the Liebenrood family. Both the east and west wings were added, together with the colonnaded portico. Numerous modifications took place over the next 100 years involving the addition of a 'porte couchere' and a decorative veranda balcony.

In 1901 the Mansion House Estate was purchased by the Reading Corporation 'for the public enjoyment'. The estate became known as Prospect Park and part of the house was used as a cafe for teas and light refreshment.

By the 1970s the house had ceased to be used even for storage and lay empty for many years.

Reading Borough Council advertised the site in 1988 and received many offers for its conversion. They were, however, attracted by ideas which retained the building for some sort of public use.

In 1989, Whitbread Plc took a long lease on the property and converted it into a Brewer's Fayre pub/restaurant.

Key points:

- The local authority was faced with the prospect of the upkeep of the Mansion House without the funds for its maintenance. They still run and maintain the park for public use.

- Whitbread offered a solution which renovated the House whilst retaining access for the public, which was much more attractive to the local authority than conversion to offices.

- Whitbread spent £2.2 million on the re-development, including the landscaping of the car park and areas adjacent to the house, to blend in with the surrounding park.

- When Whitbread bought the Grade II listed site, the building had suffered extensive fire damage and subsequent exposure to the elements had caused the roof, dome and first floor to collapse completely. Working closely with the Georgian Society and the local Civic Society, the Mansion House was restored and refurbished, paying special attention to historical information and architectural detail gathered from old plans, drawings and photographs.

- Brewer's Fayre is a branded pub/restaurant facility. Whitbread consider that many of the best sites for their pubs, restaurants and hotels which include TGI Friday's, Beefeater, Brewer's Fayre, Country Club Hotels are owned by local authorities.

Village Leisure Hotels

Boddingtons own six Village Leisure Hotels based in the North West of England. The hotels are situated in Blackpool, Bromborough, Cheadle, Hyde, Preswich and Warrington. The latest addition will be Nottingham, which will open in October 1995.

Each hotel has a large health and fitness club. Facilities differ in each hotel, but in general there is a fitness pool, gymnasium, sauna, spas, aerobics, squash and relaxation areas.

The health clubs are open to use by hotel guests and to a locally–based membership. On average, members pay a joining fee of £50/£100, with peak and off peak use costing between £23 to £39 per month. Alternatively there is a 'pay–as–you–play' charge of around £8. Clubs can take a membership of between £2,500 and £4,000 and members are queuing up to join when they open.

Key points:

- Village Leisure Hotels are an entirely privately run–company who provide additional health and fitness facilities for local communities.

- Membership fees are not excessive and membership is popular.

- By encouraging developments like Village Leisure Hotels, local authorities can increase the number of facilities available for active recreation, at no cost to themselves.

- Village Leisure Hotels were the star performer in Boddingtons annual results last year. They are looking to expand their Village Leisure group in other parts of the UK.

Partnership schemes which did not work

This book would not be complete without consideration of schemes which did not work and why they did not work.

Kingswood

Kingswood Borough Council, just outside Bristol, issued a brief for a major leisure development at Kingsfield Lane. A long list of five consortia was eventually narrowed to two with Carter Commercial and Rank Leisure/Citygrove. Initially the Council was looking for a development which included multiplex cinema, ten-pin bowling, theme bar, amusements, restaurants and a budget hotel. The aim was that these commercial leisure facilities would pay for a leisure pool and a sports hall, with an all-weather football pitch. The initial brief also required the developer to build a nuclear bunker.

The competition required the production of a model of the site, development brochures and included at least two presentations to the leisure committee. Following a public consultation period, the nightclub, amusements and budget hotel were all removed from the specification. This reduced the value of the commercial leisure and so the requirement for a leisure swimming pool was downgraded to a two-court sports hall and all-weather pitch.

Local elections and doubts over covenants on the site led to the Council withdrawing the site in 1991.

Key points:

- There was obviously considerable costs to the companies tendering for this development competition, which in the end was aborted.

- It eventually transpired that the site was owned by Avon County Council and leased to Kingswood. Unfortunately, the basis of the proposed development deal was not cleared either with the County Council or with the district auditor. The terms of the lease indicated that if the land was to be sold for commercial development then any profit would belong to the County Council. There was therefore some dispute about whether the Council would demand the value of the land from the commercial leisure development, leaving the local authority to pay for the non-commercial sport development. This was impossible, since the local authority had no capital to contribute to the scheme.

- Eventually, local elections brought about a change in the ruling political party. The new Council was against proceeding with this scheme.

Glasgow

Glasgow City Council issued a development brief for a site at Flesher's Haugh. After considerable interest was expressed by commercial leisure operators in the site, a shortlist of three consortia was drawn up.

The commercial leisure brief was for multiplex cinema, ten-pin bowling, nightclub, theme bar, amusements and restaurants. This commercial leisure would pay for leisure ice, a leisure pool and outdoor football pitches.

The shortlisted companies were required to attend a number of presentations and public meetings. Local opposition to the development of the site was so great that in due course the local authority decided to withdraw its development brief.

Key points:

- The site was situated on the edge of Glasgow adjacent to the Clyde river.

- The site was occupied by a great number of football pitches of shale or cinder. The local opposition centred around the fact that everyone in Glasgow had learned to play football on these pitches and despite the fact that a number of pitches would be replaced by better quality pitches, this well-organised opposition eventually killed the scheme.

Coventry – Pool Meadow

This city centre site for commercial leisure included the replacement of a bus station. Developers/commercial operators were required to provide multiplex cinema, ten-pin bowling, nightclub, amusements and theme bar. This scheme would provide non-commercial sports facilities of leisure ice, a refurbished restaurant in an existing building and a multi-storey car park. Some of the funding for the new bus station and the car park would come from the local bus company.

A start on site for the commercial leisure facilities was dependent on the completion of the new bus station. At this point the existing bus station could be demolished and the site developed.

While this rather complicated deal was being structured, National Amusements obtained planning permission for a multiplex cinema a five to ten minute drive away in Rugby. Commercial leisure interest in the Coventry site diminished and eventually the proposed partnership fell through.

Key points:

- The development of competing facilities over a shorter period of time killed the interest in the Coventry Site.

- Coventry City Council was hoping to use some funding raised from the sale of the site for commercial leisure for the refurbishment of the Coventry sports centre which contains a rather unique combination of two 50 metre pools. As a result of the demise of the Pool Meadow scheme, the Council has had to fund refurbishment of its sports centre from other sources.

Milton Keynes

Milton Keynes Development Corporation sold land to First Leisure Corporation for a commercial leisure development, on an understanding that they included a ice rink. Some additional land was sold to assist with a small capital contribution, but overall, First Leisure were expected to fund the ice rink from the development of ten-pin bowling and a disco and meet all its revenue charges.

In April 1993, the ice rink closed as First Leisure felt unable to fund the substantial losses of the ice skating rink since it had opened. It has since re-opened run by a private consortium.

Key points

- The amount of commercial leisure allowed on the site was not enough to fund both the capital and subsequent revenue subsidy required by the ice rink.

- The covenant with the Development Corporation meant that the ice rink had to be operated as an ice skating facility until 1995. No change of use was allowed. The ice rink could only be used for other purposes on a few days a year.

- Research published by Mintel in May 1993 showed that 35 per cent of the population in this country had never skated and 26 per cent used to go, but do not any more. 13 per cent of people do not know where their nearest ice rink is and ten per cent has been skating once, but would not go again.

- Once the Milton Keynes Development Corporation ceased to exist, Milton Keynes Borough Council were not interested in assisting with the revenue subsidy required to keep the ice rink open.

The Croydon Water Palace

In the late 1980s, The London Borough of Croydon were looking for a private sector partner to develop a leisure pool. Eventually they joined forces with Sunley Leisure who agreed to design, build and operate a Water Palace. The Council were responsible for the capital cost which included road improvements. The cost was £11.2 million.

Sunley Leisure engaged Miller Associates to undertake the design of the centre. They then undertook a design and build contract, based on the initial design.

The Waterworld comprises a large leisure pool with slides, a lazy river and some fitness swimming lanes. There is a separate health suite with weights machines.

Opened in April 1989, Sunley Leisure were contracted to run the Water Palace at no cost to the Council. Their operating subsidiary failed in August 1989 when the local authority refused to give the scheme any revenue subsidy. The London Borough of Croydon then took over the operation of the centre.

Key points:

- The London Borough of Croydon hoped that this valuable site on the main A23 road out of London would attract an investor prepared to put capital into the development of a leisure pool, as well as a partner who would be prepared to operate it. They discovered that potential investors would need some sort of planning gain for this to work and so decided to fund the capital cost of building the scheme themselves.

- A step down from a capital contribution was the proposal that, if the Council paid all the capital costs of the project, then an operator would be able to manage the centre without revenue subsidy.

- The contract was let on a design and build basis, which can be cheaper, but does have its problems if the consultant architect is not engaged to monitor the working drawings and supervise the contract on site.

- The Water Palace is now operated by the Council and it takes about 350,000 visitors each year. This is roughly equivalent of the population of the Borough, although their catchment is obviously much greater.

- The Water Palace does now just about break even in operating terms, although it does not pay back its capital.

- Quite apart from the Water Palace, there is a Council owned but privately-operated snooker and squash centre on the opposite side of the road. The site is adjacent to two hotels and near to a very broad spread of edge of town retail stores. The 'critical mass' is therefore quite attractive to invite visitors to the area who may visit the Water Palace combined with a shopping or leisure trip.

Fantaseas

In the late 1980s, two stand-alone indoor water parks were developed by Sport and Leisure Developments and their subsidiaries. The first was opened in Dartford, on a very prominent site adjacent to the entrance to the Dartford Tunnel. This site was owned by Dartford Borough Council and designated for leisure use.

Fantaseas in Dartford closed in December 1992 and was repossessed by the Local Authority.

The capital costs of the waterpark were met by the private sector developer and they were due to pay a rent to the local authority. One of the reasons why it was repossessed was because the rental had not been paid on the site for nearly two years.

Fantaseas is now subject to court action concerning the possible involvement of the local authority as guarantor for the loan, which was taken out to cover the capital cost of the waterpark. The matter is at present 'sub judice'.

Fantaseas in Chingford was built a little later, but in fact closed earlier, in 1991. It was built in a residential area, adjacent to a main road. In this instance the local authority took over the debt charge for the waterpark when the operator failed.

Key points:

- There are few, if no examples in the UK of waterparks which will repay their capital costs and make an operating profit. We will look at this issue in more detail in chapter 9.

- The operator plainly expected far greater numbers to visit these facilities than actually did so and when they did not materialise the partnership failed.

- A decision was obviously taken to provide only a waterworld. Some children felt a degree of boredom after one visit and there was nothing else on offer to create the right 'critical mass' to encourage them to use another facility or return.

- Both Councils who now own the facilities are looking to re-open and are hoping that the private sector may be interested in taking over their operation. It is quite likely that a partner will be found and there is no reason why in the long term, both waterworlds should not be operated successfully. The unfortunately consequence of this failure is that someone else has had to pick up the cost of funding the initial capital development for these schemes.

The Plaza at Exeter

This was one of the first attempts at a partnership between a private sector developer and a local authority in the UK. Rush & Tompkins took over a small local developer in Exeter who were developing a site for a J Sainsbury superstore and a sports centre. The site was owned by the City Council and leased for 125 years to J Sainsbury. The leisure centre was to be funded from the planning gain arising out of the sale of land to the superstore.

Initially, the leisure centre was to have been handed over to the local authority once it was built and the local authority would then have been responsible for operating it.

Rush & Tompkins (R & T) decided that they would invest some capital funding in the project themselves and operate it as a private sector facility.

The Plaza contains a early design of a leisure pool with a flume, snooker hall, theme bar, health suite, saunas, small gym, 4 squash courts, amusements, one and half court sports hall with spectator seating for 1500 and a street café to be used in conjunction with Sainsburys. The cost of the leisure facilities was between £5-8 million.

Unfortunately for R & T, the initial deal was carried out with a particular council in Exeter, but even before the project was completed, local authority political control changed and the in-coming party were not prepared to co-operate with R & T. Agreement for change of use of facilities were refused and R & T were left with a facility which they had to operate under the initial agreement they had signed.

In due course, Rush & Tompkins went into liquidation and the lease for the site then reverted to Sainsburys.

J Sainsbury then engaged Sports Partner (the consultant arm of the Sports Council Trust) to advise them on appointing a private sector operator. The Plaza is now operated by City Centre Leisure, under an agreed contract with Sainsburys.

Key points:

- Local authorities have held up the Plaza in the past as a failed partnership and therefore a reason why they should not become involved with the private sector.

- It must be remembered that the Plaza was a very early example of partnership in 1984, at the height of the property boom. At that time developers and operators were prepared to believe that sports facilities could make a far greater return on capital and revenue employed than is understood today.

- It was unfortunate that early co-operation with the local authority disintegrated with a change in political colour. It is very difficult to make any partnership work if the local authority is against it.

Notes and references

1. Facilities Planning Model, contained in *Planning and Provision for Sport Fact File*, available from the Sports Council. £15.

2. The Indoor Tennis Initiative — The Lawn Tennis Association 071 385 2366.

3. *Planning Obligations for Sport and Recreation, A guide for Negotiation and Action*, published by The Sports Council £25.00.

7

Examples of partnership with CCT which offer revenue and capital funding

Introduction

If you were looking for one reason why there are misunderstandings between local authorities and the private sector about partnership arrangements, it would be Compulsory Competitive Tendering (CCT). It is the aim of this chapter to look at the historical problems surrounding the introduction of CCT and to examine case studies of where the private sector is able to invest capital and revenue funding into centres which they operate. This may be through voluntary arrangements with local authorities or through the process of bidding for CCT contracts.

Looking back to the initial opposition of local authorities to the introduction of CCT, it is hard to separate the real aims of the Government in introducing this legislation from their publicly avowed aims. Equally, it is difficult to separate the real aims of the Government from their presumed aims, which were the subject of endless speculation by the leisure press and by local authorities. Publicly, the Government wished to encourage competition by asking private sector contractors to bid for the management of local authority sport and leisure centres. Local authorities saw this as a way of ending public funding for the provision of sport and leisure facilities in their communities. It is more likely that the Government's real aim was to improve the service of local authorities to their local communities and to achieve better value for money. It did, however, introduce an antipathy of local authorities to the private sector which took some years to overcome.

One reason for this antipathy was the misunderstanding that private sector companies, particularly those in the commercial leisure industry, would be fighting to take over local authority owned sport and leisure centres. Even Central Government expected far more interest from the private sector than eventually transpired. However, when it was first introduced, most of the large leisure owner-operators made it clear that the terms on which the Government were offering contracts to the private sector were of little interest.

One reason for this lack of interest was the relative viability of sport and leisure centres under local authority control. There was little understanding of the high costs of operating swimming pools (plant is always expensive to maintain), or the costs of running a sports hall, which can often only be used by a few people at any one time. The requirement for a continued operating subsidy from the local authority inevitably decreased its interest to large leisure operators.

Equally important to the private sector was the short five year management contracts on offer and the lack of any opportunity to buy the leisure centre. As discussed in previous chapters, most private sector operators of commercial leisure facilities are 'owner-operators'. They tend to own most of the land on which they operate, or if they do not own the land, it will be leased on a long lease of 25 years plus. CCT offered only five year operating contracts and that provided few incentives for capital investment.

Finally, it also become clear that 'management contracts' were of little interest to large leisure operators, because they had little experience of managing the type of facility they were being asked to operate. Management of ten-pin bowling or a nightclub or a pub as a commercial concern is very different from managing a swimming pool at subsided rates. Altogether, CCT contracts was a package unlikely to attract investment from large leisure companies, they were much more likely to be of interest to a slightly smaller company, or a large company which specialised in managing contracts for the public sector.

In retrospect, nearly 50 per cent of all CCT contracts won by the private sector have been taken up by companies who only manage a single facility. The rest have been taken up by a handful of companies which do indeed specialise in the management of public sector contracts. Many of these companies like Serco have previous experience of running other local authority CCT contracts such as grounds maintenance or refuse collection.

In 1993, a study completed by Leisure Futures was published. This assessed the relative improvement in standards of service of centres operated by Direct Service Organisations (DSOs) — the in-house organisation of the local authority and those operated by private sector companies. Not surprisingly, they concluded that there was little to chose between them. Good management has never been the prerogative of working in the private or public sectors.

A study commissioned by the Sports Council from the Centre for Leisure Research in Edinburgh,[1] assessed the depth of interests shown by the private sector in the first tranche of contracts which were let between 1990 and 1992. The report showed that 50 per cent of contracts operated by the private sector were won by small single operating companies. Indeed, only 55 per cent of contracts offered up by local authorities managed to invite three bidders, which was the suggested minimum in the CCT legislation. 92 per cent of local authorities invited two or more bids, but 60 per cent of local authorities awarded their contract to their DSO unopposed. Looking at the size of the contracts operated by private sector companies, some 80 per cent of contracts for £1 million plus were uncontested. The conclusion is that the CCT market for sport and leisure is dominated by two types of commercial operator: the first is a small company interested in operating a single facility in its local area. The second is the larger company that specialised in the management of local authority contracts and operates contracts for perhaps 12 different local authorities. Most of all the contracts operated by the private sector are concentrated in the Midlands and South. No contracts are operated by large commercial leisure operators.

Looking at all this from a private sector perspective, it becomes clear that the operation of CCT contracts by the private sector can and does work well, but only when the local authority has a will to make it work. It is interesting that 39 per cent of all contracts operated by the private sector were set up before CCT was introduced — they are voluntary arrangements, not compulsory. As we will see from the case studies in this chapter, where the local authority has a will to make co-operation with the private sector work, then it works and works well. The private sector can reduce the revenue subsidies previously required from the local authority and they can and do invest capital into the centres they operate, in return for variations to or extended contracts.

It is also fair to say, however, that where the local authority is determined to fight off any bid from the private sector to run their facility, then this is relatively easy. They could, for example, advertise contracts in obscure publications to ensure that no outside bids are submitted. Although there are guidelines laid down by DoE on the information that should be required from the private sector when making their bid, some specifications laid out by local authority teams run to volume after volume. The cost of submitting bids can be artificially enhanced out of all proportion. DoE has also shown little sign of responding in a positive way to any complaints made of anti-competitive behaviour.

The returns for private sector companies operating in this area can be small and as companies like Crossland discovered in the early days of CCT, over–expansion can be difficult to control in an area where returns are limited. When the first CCT contracts were awarded it took time for new private sector companies to set up the right structures and organisations with which to bid. They then had to cope with the demands of bidding for so many contracts over a relatively short space of time. This may well change in the future and there are several 'watchers' of the CCT market who believe that there will be substantial additional interest from the private sector when the contracts come up for renewal. This infant industry has acquired much greater experience and has learned which contracts to go for and which to leave alone. Many contractors have learned to read between the lines and know that when a local authority felt forced to tender because of the 'C' (compulsory) in CCT, then there was little point in the private sector bidding at all.

In the future, where the private sector already operate a contract, it is quite possible that the option of a 'DSO' bid no longer exists. Alternatively, there are some DSOs who are struggling to fulfil the contract which they won. One private sector contractor bid for a contract offering £1 million less than the cost of the existing contract to the local authority. They lost to the DSO who bid to reduce the costs by £2 million. Is the DSO really going to run the contract at £2 million less than it did before CCT was introduced and if it is, why did it not do so in the first place? Some local authorities are realising that their DSO does not have the experience to fulfil the terms of their contracts. Either they look for help, or they hide these the additional costs somewhere else within the authorities' budget.

An alternative view is that the existing DSOs have become more efficient throughout the operation of their first contract. The private sector may find themselves with more opposition the second time round.

The requirement by local authorities to reduce their revenue costs and indeed attract capital investment from the private sector may make a private sector contractor more attractive as a partner the second time round, even if the first time the local authority was determined to manage the facility itself.

There are, however, some additional headaches like the European Community Acquired Rights Directive. This Directive dates back to 1977 and was framed with company takeovers in mind. Where the Directive applies, a company is required to take over the contract of existing staff on their existing wages and conditions. It was not anticipated that the Directive would include contracting–out of services. However, over the past few years, a series of European Court cases has extended the Directive's application and generated uncertainty about what constitutes a 'relevant transfer of an undertaking' which causes the Directive to apply. The Court cases have indicated that the Directive can apply to CCT, but it is not clear when. Each case must be judged individually. The Government is pressing for the Directive to be amended to clarify its application. In the meanwhile it must be followed as it currently stands.

The Directive was implemented into UK law by the Transfer of Undertakings (Protection of Employment) Regulations 1981 (TUPE). The confusion created by the European Court cases applies to TUPE as well: i.e. it is not clear when TUPE is appropriate. In March 1993 the Government issued guidance on the factors to be considered when assessing whether or not a transaction may involve a transfer of an undertaking. At the same time a statement by the Secretary of State for the Environment gave guidance on TUPE and CCT. DoE Circular 10/93 issued in June 1993 and a paper circulated to local authorities in January this year gave further guidance.

Whether TUPE applies depends on both the nature of the service to be contracted out and on contractor's proposals for carrying it out. TUPE may apply to one set of proposals, but not to another. Contractors are free to bid on a TUPE or non-TUPE basis. They should take a view as to whether TUPE will apply to their proposals and price accordingly. Having seen the bids, the local authority will also take a view on TUPE. DoE has issued advice on how to proceed in cases where there is disagreement.

So, where partnerships have and do exist, what examples are there of good practice which might encourage local authorities to seek potential interest from the private sector to operate their sport and leisure centre?

Case studies

Epsom & Ewell

The Rainbow sport and leisure centre comprises a 25 m swimming pool and learner pool, sports hall, indoor bowls and cafe. The local authority let the contract on 1st January 1992 to Civic Leisure, who are the management contract arm of Archer Leisure (formerly Queens Moat Leisure). In return for an extended contract, Civic Leisure invested £300,000 in new facilities. This provided an upgraded crèche to meet new government guidelines, a power weights gym, Dojo martial arts centre, a dance studio and hi-tech fitness gymnasium.

Key points:

- this contract began in January 1992 and will finish in December 1995. The capital investment by Civic has therefore been achieved through variations to the contract, rather than an extension. In other words, it is not always necessary to extend a contract beyond the five or six years to attract capital investment. Variations which allow the private sector partner to take more of the revenue from the initial contract can provide an alternative answer.

- through the capital injection provided by Civic Leisure, the local authority have improved their facilities, without using any of their own capital. At the end of the contract they will own, without obligation, the new facilities.

- through the introduction of the new facilities, usage and throughput for the centre is increased.

- the capital invested does not increase the deficit funding required from the Council. It is more likely that the contractor will make his return by taking the income from the new facilities for the duration of the contract, but it is also likely that there will be an increased profit share for the local authority, caused by the increased usage of the centre.

- variations to contracts will allow capital investment by a private sector operator, but the investment is limited by the return achievable during the life of the contract. A longer contract will allow for more investment in facilities such as changing rooms, which will show a return over a number of years, but are difficult to make profitable over four or five years.

Broxbourne

Broxbourne Borough Council had a 25 m pool and learner pool which was built in 1986. They then decided to invest in dry sports and a sports hall, health suite, sports injury clinic, 4 squash courts, crèche, outdoor sports pitch, meeting room and café and bar were added in 1989/90. Civic Leisure took over the contract on 1 January 1990 and have invested capital of £270,000 in a health suite, gymnasium, re-surfacing outdoor tennis courts, and a new computer booking system.

Key points

- the contract began in January 1990 and will finish in December 1994. The contract was set up as a voluntary arrangement before tendering became compulsory.

- no DSO bid for the contract, so it was written into the tender that bids could include a capital investment Part of the bid from Civic Leisure included a promise to invest £200,000 in the contract. In reality, an additional £70,000 has now been invested.

- the increased usage of this centre has meant that in the third year, 1993, Civic Leisure has returned an increase in performance of over 50 per cent in shared profit for the local authority.

- the key issues given under the Epsom and Ewell project also apply to Broxbourne.

- the local authority is currently preparing new documentation for the contract to go out to tender for a second time at the end of 1994.

Westminster City Council

Civic Leisure operated three centres for Westminster City Council. The Porchester Centre contains two pools, 33 metre and large learner pool, the largest Russian and Turkish Baths in the UK (known as the Porchester Spa), 2 squash courts, small gym, slipper baths. Civic Leisure have invested in a new gymnasium snooker room and sunbeds.

At Marshal Street a large 33 metre pool has been complemented by a new gymnasium with weights and cardiovascular equipment, dance studio and health suite.

The Jubilee Centre is a traditional local authority run centre with 25 metre pool, one court sports hall and cafe. Due to the large number of cafes in the area, this space in the Jubilee Centre has been converted to a fitness factory, gymnasium and crèche.

Key points:

- the original five year contract was extended by one year and will finish at the end of 1994.

- Civic Leisure have invested over £500,000 in capital over the life of the contract.

- over five years, £95,000 has been paid over to Westminster City Council in over-performance fees.

- Westminster City Council retained the right to participate in planned capital funding. Facilities like sunbeds which were jointly funded by the partnership has returned over £75,000 to the City Council.

- the contract has saved Westminster City Council over £3 million over the life of the contract. This figure is estimated by comparing the usage of the existing centres before the contract began with the increased usage and the capital invested.

South Oxford District Council

The Wave leisure pool at Didcot is managed by the Relaxion Group Plc, who are a management buyout (MBO) of St Albans Leisure. The pool, which opened in February 1992, is operated by Relaxion on a ten year contract. In return for an extended contract Relaxion have invested £150,000 in the fitting out of a Harpers cardio/vascular gymnasium.

Key points:

- this is a good example of an extended contract in return for capital investment by the private sector partner.

- as a modern leisure pool, it is expected to break even. If it makes a profit or a loss then this is borne or taken by Relaxion.

Salisbury Leisure Centre

Salisbury District Council own a dry sports centre with a two-court sports hall and 3 squash courts. In 1992, Relaxion Group won the tender to manage the facility. They then negotiated a ten year extension to their original four year contract, in return for investing £150,000-£200,000 for the refurbishment of the bar and the creation of a Harpers branded fitness facility.

Relaxion take the profit from the new facilities. They, however, also manage a new athletics track and hockey pitch adjacent to the sports centre, which was not built when the CCT contract was first let. All takings from these facilities are returned to the local authority.

Key points:

- Salisbury District Council own two other wet facilities within their control. The contract to run one centre was won by the DSO. The second centre is a dual-use site and so not subject to CCT.

- although the local authority do not receive any increased revenue from the improved facilities during the ten year life of the contract, they will end up with improved facilities and throughput of users when the contract is put out to tender at the end of 14 years.

St Albans

In 1991, St Albans City and District Council Leisure Services Department was subject to a management buyout, led by its Director, John McGinley. From 1 June 1991, the newly formed management company called St Albans Leisure Limited, which subsequently became part of Relaxion Group Plc, had a five year contract for the management and operation of most of the Council's sport and leisure amenities, with the exception of the Museums service. This includes four sports centres, tennis centre, golf courses, Alban Arena, Maltings Arts Centre, public halls (with one exception), Tourism Information Centre and children's playgrounds and the bookings of all sports pitches. The local authority continues to own all the premises, control pricing policies and supervise the contract.

At London Colney, Hertfordshire County Council closed a school premises, and responsibility for the school sports facilities, which comprised a gymnasium, changing rooms and associated classrooms and outdoor tennis courts, passed to the local authority. The local authority refurbished the classrooms and created a health and fitness facility with aerobics hall. The centre was underused and the one badminton court–sized gym was used almost exclusively for five-a-side football and badminton

When St Albans Leisure took over the contract, they invested £170,000-180,000 in converting the gym to a children's adventure world. The changing rooms were converted to a café and a walk through connected the reception area with all other facilities.

Key points:

- St Albans Leisure have a five year contract for this centre. Under the management buy-out agreement, the Council will pay St Albans Leisure Limited a deficit fee and the company returns a royalty on income to the Council. The local authority therefore benefits immediately from the increased revenue which these new facilities will generate.

- the Adventure World is a new concept which offers children up to the age of 14 an indoor soft play activity area. It is equipped with swings, slides, ropes, ball pools, PVC shapes, punch bags and other features which offer hours of entertainment. Certain features include sound effects — mobiles will squawk or clouds squeak when hit with soft balls. There is a separate area for the under fives and parents can watch from the café area, or during certain times in the day join their children.

Cherwell District Council

Cherwell District Council had an existing outdoor 50 metre pool and community centre and were without funds either to refurbish these facilities, or to add any new ones. The population of Cherwell is approximately 41,000, although their catchment is larger when the population of the nearby town of Daventry is taken into account.

The Council established a unique three-way partnership. They set up a limited company without share capital, in which £1 shares were held by the local authority (19 per cent), members of the local community representing the users of the centre such as the swimming pool club and a new formed bowls club and a private sector company, (Serco) who would manage the completed project. The limited company borrowed £750,000 which was necessary to refurbish the existing facilities and to build a new build indoor bowls hall. The completed centre is managed on a 15 year contract by the private sector CCT operator, Serco.

Key points

- the Council did not have sufficient expendable capital to undertake the project. They did, however, find a way to act as a true 'enabler' to improve the sports facilities for the local community.

- the local authority did, on the other hand, have the ability to increase the existing revenue support given annually to this centre.

- in setting up this project, the Council had five main aims: to attract a commercial partner; to achieve an off-balance sheet investment; to involve the local community in the running of the project; to achieve fixed revenue costs and to build an indoor bowls facility.

- by setting up a bank loan, with guaranteed interest payment met from the revenue budget available from the local authority, Serco were able to participate and facilitate this scheme.

- a comprehensive business plan identified the cost of repaying the loan, maintenance costs and deficit funding required for the completed scheme over the 15 year life of the partnership. The Council are therefore in a position to know exactly what revenue funding is required for this centre for the next fifteen years.

- the loan was made on the basis of a guaranteed receivable stream, rather than on asset security, based on a business plan. The Council retains land ownership and the centre passes over to their control after 15 years. The annual revenue subsidy from the Council is responsible for paying the bank loan and for covering any revenue deficit in running the centre. Serco are able to make their profit from the management fee.

- by refurbishing the centre and adding indoor bowls, the annual operating costs of the scheme were reduced, therefore reducing the sum which the Council had to make available for maintenance. The slightly more commercial nature of the new indoor bowls hall produces a slight surplus which can cross-subsidise the other less commercial facilities.

- this complicated, but unique solution took 2.5 to 3 years to achieve. It is, however, a very good example of a local authority working with a private sector company to a achieve a partnership where the aspirations of both are satisfied.

Richmond Pool

The Richmond Pool on the main A316 was first opened in June 1966. It is owned by the London Borough of Richmond–upon–Thames and built on land leased from the Crown Commissioners.

In 1986, a commercial operator, built and operated adjacent to the pool the first flume complex to be built in the UK. The facility was, however, closed following a fatal accident in 1987.

In the late 1980s, Richmond–upon–Thames was involved in a re-development scheme with LET Leisure, which would involve the demolition of the pool and its replacement by a commercial leisure complex. This would have included an ice rink and replacement swimming pool. The scheme was linked with the closure of the existing Richmond ice rink, which was on a site owned by LET Leisure. It was proposed that this site be redeveloped for housing.

Unfortunately, the LET proposal for the Richmond pool site fell through when time ran out on a right of way agreement with an adjoining user. The ice rink was closed and LET Leisure paid Richmond Council £2.4 million by way of a penalty, in view of their failure to build a replacement within the agreed time limit. Although there was much criticism of the Council's original granting of planning permission for the rink's demolition, they had been advised by a leading QC that they had little option, as it was very likely that LET would have a refusal overturned on appeal. In that event the Council would have achieved no money from LET.

By late 1990, it was clear that the Richmond pool needed urgent refurbishment and a technical survey carried out by the Council gave a preliminary cost for a basic refurbishment of £1.6 million. In June 1991, it was decided to proceed with the refurbishment, programmed in two phases, but the Council decided to look around for a partner to provide a possible additional investment.

In August 1991, Whitewater Leisure were appointed manager of the facility for one year while they prepared proposals to the Council for refurbishment. These proposals were presented in January 1992 and then put out to public consultation.

Whitewater Leisure invested an additional £950,000 which was added to the Council's contribution of £1.6 million for a total project cost of £2.55 million. In return Whitewater were offered a 15 year contract for a annual management fee of £303,000 which represented a saving on the cost of operating the pool directly by the Council.

The Original facilities on the site include a 33.3 yard indoor swimming pool and a teaching pool, plus a 33.3 yard outdoor swimming pool. New facilities which have been added as part of the refurbishment programme include a health and fitness suite, weight training centre, dance studio, restaurant cafe and information technology system. The second phase of the programme will add a children's crèche and adventure area. The refurbishment has included a new roof and plant, replaced glazing and seating and the demolition of the flumes.

Key points:

- in a similar way to Parkside Cambridge, the Richmond site is sensitive. The site is owned by the Crown Commissioners and held on a lease by the Council until 2016. Options to enter into partnership with commercial leisure operators were limited by likely traffic congestion, the site's history and fears of over development. The site contains 33 metres indoor and outdoor pools and any suggestion to shut this facility would be fiercely opposed by the local community.

- throughout the refurbishment a Consultation Group (representing local interests) supported by two Councillors from the Leisure Services Committee met regularly to comment on the scheme as it was developed. In addition, information bulletins were issued on the progress of the contract, which have been made available in public libraries.

- the authorities' rates support grant is allocated on the historic expenditure patterns based on the low spending in the 1970s. Therefore, the ability to spend new capital from 1990s resources are severely limited. Capital controls would not allow the authority to raise the additional funds through borrowing.

- through the partnership with Whitewater, the Council has achieved a more extensive refurbishment and redevelopment of the pool than would have been possible on its own. It has also frozen its revenue subsidy to the pool based on the £303,000 required in 1991/92. They are now in a position to know that this figure and no more, will be required on an annual basis for the next 15 years.

- Whitewater have to cover the £950,000 funding out of the £303,000 they are paid as a revenue subsidy. They also have to take their management fee out of this subsidy and make a profit. There is therefore a strong incentive for them to cut the costs of running the building and to achieve increased revenue from the new facilities added.

- since re-opening as 'Pools on the Park', attendances have more than doubled and a MORI poll has shown that satisfaction with swimming pools in the Borough has increased by 23 per cent.

Weston-super-Mare

Woodspring District Council advertised for a private sector partner to invest capital and operate the Tropicana outdoor leisure pool on the seafront of Weston-super-Mare.

A number of bids were received and Contemporary Leisure won the contract. In return for a 21 year lease, Contemporary will invest £1 million within the first three years and are paying a rent for the site. The local authority estimate that they will achieve savings of £150,000 from their revenue budget.

Key points:

- the local authority considered looking for a partner for CCT, but decided that this option provided little or no incentive to invest in improved facilities.

- the outdoor pool required annual revenue subsidy and needed capital investment. By attracting a private sector partner, the local authority was no longer required to provide either capital or revenue funding.

- £300,000 has been invested by Contemporary Leisure during phase 1 for a refurbished bar and cafe area. Over the next two years, it is anticipated that changing accommodation will be refurbished and some sort of temporary roof cover added for use when it rains.

- it is important in areas which attract tourists that the provision of sport and leisure facilities can be used as a draw to extend the season. By providing some sort of cover for the pool and refurbishing the facilities, it hoped that the pool can remain open continuously between Easter and October.

Notes and references

1. *Sport and Leisure Management — Compulsory Competitive Tendering National Information Report*, available from the Sports Council, £15.

8

Other examples of partnership for revenue funding

As we have examined in previous chapters, although capital spending by local authorities presents them with a great problems, pressure on revenue funding for sports and leisure facilities is increasingly coming under the microscope. Central Government controls, pressures to increase spending in areas which are a statutory duty and overall reductions in a local authority's income forces leisure and recreation departments to look elsewhere for ways of enhancing their income.

Sponsorship has always been at the top of the list and local companies have always been approached to support local events. Sports companies like Carlton may sponsor a badminton competition, or a local car dealer or newspaper may be prepared to sponsor an event. As the recession bit in the late 1980s, support of this nature has been declining. Local authority leisure departments found themselves fighting for local sponsorship and competing against other departments within the local authority. The London Borough of Sutton investigated the development of a formalised partnership approach to the private sector and identified that there were certain companies in the Borough who were repeatedly approached by the Council. This identified how important it was that these companies were not constantly overwhelmed by approaches for sponsorship. There were occasions when the same company was approached by different council departments, which created a poor impression, showing a lack of corporate co-ordination which often resulted in a loss of potential sponsorship. Another local authority leisure department set up a fairly innovative scheme whereby employees were given a bonus of ten per cent if they attracted outside sponsorship for events. They raised more in six months than they had over the previous six years, until the district auditor pointed out that since their contracts stated that attracting sponsorship was part of their job description, then they could not be offered a bonus on top!

Sponsorship for sport was given a much needed boost by the announcement in November 1992 of the Government funded Sportsmatch Scheme.

Sportsmatch

Sportsmatch is aimed at grass roots sponsorship of sport and is very much based on the successful ABSA scheme for Business Sponsorship of the Arts. In England £3.3 million per annum is available, administered by the Institute of Sports Sponsorship.[1] In Scotland the pot holds £500,000 per year and in Wales £247,000. Launched in November 1992, Sportsmatch has supported nearly 400 sponsorships covering 50 sports. £6.8 million has been generated by these grants for sports sponsorship.

The idea of Sportsmatch is that it will match the funds put up by a sponsor for an event or even for a building, offering a minimum of £1,000 and a maximum of £75,000. All bids are assessed by an Awards Panel and bids have to be received at least 12 weeks before the event. Sponsorship cannot be retrospective — so there is no point in holding an event and then hoping that Sportsmatch will cover the deficit!

Quite apart from sponsorship of an event or a sport team, there is beginning to be a growth of companies interested in putting their names to a building. In Kettering, the Leisure Village has sponsorship from Weetabix for their tennis centre (Weetabix is a locally–based company) and from Pepsi for their ice rink (see page 42 for further details). Norwich Sports Village has its flumes sponsored by Mars.

There is potential for using sponsorship as a means of reducing the revenue support of a council for an event or a building.

Sport and its role in the community

In Chapter 2, we discussed the role of sport in urban regeneration and in City Challenge. That chapter concentrated on partnerships for the building of facilities in inner city areas, rather than on its role for encouraging participation. There is no doubt that sports facilities should be part of the infrastructure of inner city regeneration, along with new roads, and local shops and supermarkets. Sport does, however, have a major role to play in the day–to–day life of the community in encouraging young people to participate in sports activities and through sport development.

There is nothing particularly new about the concept of local authorities working with the Sports Council to work with the disadvantaged, and even young offenders, through sport. In the early 1980s, the Sports Council set up a scheme in Portsmouth and Southampton with the Magistrates Court called 'Solent Sports Counselling'. This scheme looked at young people at risk of offending and even those who had offended and introduced them to sport development. Research conducted over a three to five year period of the project identified that 50 per cent of young offenders helped by the scheme did not re-offend. In due course, when funding from the Sports Council came to an end, the Hampshire Probation Service took on the project.

However, in the 1990s, many of these schemes are looking for support not only from the Sports Council, but also from the private sector and one of the most unique partnerships which exists between a local authority and the private sector is the Croydon Sports Partnership:

The Croydon Sports Partnership [2]

The Croydon Sports Partnership was conceived as a response to the inner-city riots of the early to mid–eighties. There was a perceived lack of opportunities existing in many inner-city areas for young people to take part in challenging and constructive activities and the Sports Development concept was developed as the way forward.

The Partnership has developed as an excellent example of public and private sector co-operation. It has taken over the role of Sports Development from the local authority and 50 per cent of its funds comes from local private sector companies, led by Nestlé. Close and constructive working relationships have been built with the local authority and its many departments, as well as with the local schools, who welcome the initiative and make their facilities available for the Partnership's use.

The Croydon Sports Partnership offers some 16 different sports with development through schools and through courses out of school hours and in holidays. There is close co-operation with the Governing bodies of sport and the London Region of The Sports Council and particular assistance is offered to the more disadvantaged and people with disabilities. In 1992 attendance at courses rose to nearly 10,000 people who were offered 'taster' sessions, organised and supervised sport activity sessions, competitions, coaching, training and leadership courses and above all specialised help and advice. Trustees are split between the Council who have three nominees, the business supporters who have three members and sporting clubs.

The Partnership is a company limited by guarantee with charitable status and is unique in what it offers to the local community, local businesses and the London Borough of Croydon. For further information about charitable status see chapter 10.

The Youth Charter for Sport [3]

In some local authorities, sport development is well funded and imaginative. In other local authorities it does not exist at all. The Sports Council and other bodies like the National Coaching Foundation work hard to encourage sports development in pursuit of excellence. Less well publicised is their work for the sports development at a community level and only now, as the law and order problems faced by this country are increasing, is the role of sport in tackling the causes of those problems being acknowledged.

Geoff Thompson is the former five times World Karate Champion and the Chairman of the North West Region of The Sports Aid Foundation. He is also an independent member of The Sports Council. Originally from the east end of London, Geoff is now settled in Manchester and very involved in offering sport as a means of bridging the gap between the ganglands of Moss Side and other inner city areas of Manchester and as the way forward for personal development in life. In March 1993, Geoff launched the Youth Charter at the Recreation Management Conference at Wembley. This was followed by a British/American Chamber sponsored visit by twenty young people from the Los Angeles who in response to the riots there in 1992, formed an initiative called 'The Spirit of Los Angeles'. All the youngsters came from deprived backgrounds and were members of a special youth task force getting involved in front-line community projects. Hosted by The Sports Council, these young people came to see what they could learn from the British inner-city experience.

Towards the end of 1993, BISL joined in partnership with Geoff Thompson to bring the Youth Charter scheme to fruition. The Youth Charter has several principle aims:

- To establish a national platform for youth and sport.

- To work with communities to create opportunities for young people and to encourage personal development through sport, regardless of colour creed or ability.

- To encourage business, both locally or at national level to invest in young people through the provision and support of opportunities for sport in local communities.

- To involve sports personalities to act as role models for young people.

- To encourage a positive commitment to school, identifying the benefits and opportunities of a continued education.

- To encourage young people to work towards qualifications to be gained from an active involvement in sport. For example, Community Sport Leader Awards, Duke of Edinburgh Awards and National Vocational Qualifications.

- To encourage from an early age the benefits of a continued active, healthy lifestyle.

- To encourage young people to work together through sport for themselves and their communities.

Support has been gathered from the British Urban Regeneration Association (BURA) and Business In The Community (BITC). This group has been joined by the Metropolitan Police. At the time of writing, the Youth Charter aims to set up two pilot projects in the North West of England and in London. Bolton Metropolitan Borough Council already have schemes which involve their sport development department in working with young drug addicts and young offenders. In 1993, a youth games in Moss Side allowed police into an area for the first time in years.

The Youth Charter will offer companies the opportunity to sponsor sports personalities. Various organisations like Business In The Community through its Aim High programme have tried using business leaders as role models. The difficulty is that unless you are Richard

Branson, it is hard for a young person at school to relate to the achievement of business men and women. Sport falls into another category altogether. The death in the past year of Arthur Ashe, Bobby Moore and Sir Matt Busby received more press and media coverage than the death of any business man or even former heads of state. Anyone who has any interest in sport and many people who have no interest, can appreciate the attraction and place in their lives of those who excel at sport. Many sports personalities such as Geoff Thompson are acutely aware of this and already the Youth Charter has the support of leading sportsmen and women such as:

Fatima Whitbread	David Wilkie
Johny Searle	Greg Searle
Colin Jackson	Judy Simpson
Nick Faldo	Chris Boardman
Lenny Paul	Eugene Gilkes
Lindford Christie	Cindy Gilbert
Tessa Sanderson	

The way the Youth Charter will work is that companies will be asked to sponsor an athlete (to use a generic term to cover all sportsmen and women). Obviously the level of sponsorship will influence who is made available. The sponsor will then be able to use the sports personality for appearances at company events and promotions, but part of the funds from the sponsorship will be used for the sports personality to work in the local community. For local companies, sponsorship may assist young up–and–coming sports people who no one has heard of nationally, but who are, or who are becoming well known in their local community. An athlete may chose to adopt a school in the area where he lives or where he comes from. If successful, the Youth Charter could become a national partnership scheme which draws together the business community, with its sports community and local schools.

The Youth Charter will lock into other schemes which exist. In 1993, the Government announced that grants of up to £20,000 (average grant £15,000) would be offered to the top 100 athletes through the Sports Aid Foundation and the Foundation for Sport and the Arts to help with training running up to the next Olympics. All athletes who are to be funded through this scheme have been approached and asked if they will offer some community appearances in return for this sponsorship. It may well be that the Youth Charter can fit in with these arrangements.

There are a whole range of charitable trusts which offer activity based assistance to disadvantaged groups. All could benefit from the Youth Charter. At this stage, it is probably worth highlighting the work of the Duke of Edinburgh's Award who has set up a very imaginative partnership scheme 'The Charter for Business' of its own.

The Duke of Edinburgh's Award – The Charter for Business [4]

The Duke of Edinburgh's Award began in 1956 and offers young people between the age of 14 and 25 an opportunity to experience challenge and adventure, acquire new skills and make new friends. There are three levels of the Award: Bronze, Silver and Gold. To gain any of these levels, each young entrant must complete four sections: Expeditions/Explorations; Skills; Physical Recreation and Service. The award is taken up by around 12 per cent of all 14 to 16 year olds, with around 200,000 young people taking part each year, with the assistance of 50,000 voluntary helpers. Over two million young people have taken up the challenge of the Scheme since it began and the Award Scheme is operated across the world in 58 countries.

In May 1992, the Award took a major change in direction and launched the 'Charter for Business' — a programme designed to spearhead the Award's drive to business. The Charter began with the support of ten of Britain's leading companies, aiming to recruit 100,000 young people to begin their gold and Silver Awards. Since then, more than 50 companies have joined the 'Charter for Business', pledging sponsorship over a five year period. This partnership with the private sector has two main objectives. For companies who participate, there is an opportunity to use the Award for employees as part of their overall training programme. In the words of the Organisational Development Manager of British Aerospace, the Duke of Edinburgh's Award is *"probably the most cost effective form of management development we've ever been able to take"*. The Award can be used as a tool for developing drive, initiative, commitment and self-confidence. Pubmaster, part of the Brent Walker Group, are Charter Members and have identified various pubs as centres where Award members can meet. They also appreciate the possibilities for encouraging young people who visit their pubs to participate in the Award.

The second objective of involving the private sector in the Award is to raise funds — approximately £1 million in the first year of The Charter for Business, for work with the disadvantaged. It is interesting that many of the 10,000 operating units for the Award are through Youth Departments in County and Metropolitan Councils, rather than through leisure and recreation departments in District Authorities. Perhaps this will change with the advent of unitary authorities — there is obviously a connection between the work of leisure departments encouraging more people to use their sport and leisure centres and the expedition and physical recreation section of the Award. The Award Scheme has in a number of areas become established as a means of building respect and a sense of responsibility among young offenders. Groups are run in free time for those in detention centres. The Award seeks to work with young people in rural areas — attracting problems of isolation, difficulties with transport and limitations on the variety of options which are open to young people. The Award is of obvious benefit to young people whose self-confidence has been eroded and can for the unemployed be the first step towards getting a job. In inner city areas, the Award has launched a number of projects, often with the support of local industry in seconding staff.

There are opportunities for partnership arrangements with schemes for young people like the Duke of Edinburgh's Award which can bring more people into our sport and leisure centre and it is an area which needs more investigation.

If sport and leisure and, in particular, sport and leisure departments within local authorities are to fulfil their true potential, sport has to be looked at as a tool with wider applications. We are no longer in a situation where we can sit back and say, well, here are the sports facilities — come and use them. (Many local authorities would dispute that this has ever been the case and that sports development has been a priority, in co-operation with the Sports Council for many years.) What perhaps is more important now is partnership at all levels. Partnership can assist with capital funding, but equally, if used correctly, it can also assist with revenue provision. If law and order is one area where sport has a role to play in tackling the causes and giving young people another outlet for their energy, equally important is the role sport has to play in the 'Health of the Nation'.

The Allied Dunbar National Fitness Survey [5]

A good example of partnership in its own right, the National Fitness Survey was the idea of DNH, the Sports Council, the Department of Health and the Health Education Authority who persuaded Allied Dunbar to provide additional sponsorship to the funding they raised between them. Between February and November 1990, a survey was carried out on a representative sample of 6,000 adults (16 years of age and over), throughout England. A total of 4,316 people completed the home interview stage — a response rate of 75 per cent. 70 per cent of those interviewed took part in a physical appraisal with 62 per cent attending for tests at a specially equipped mobile laboratory and 8 per cent primarily the more elderly and infirm, being tested on reduced set of measurements in their home.

The survey measured many aspects of behaviour, attitudes and beliefs. These included levels of participation in sport, physical activity at work, at home and in moving about, other lifestyle and health-related behaviour, including smoking and drinking, current health status, sports-related injuries, knowledge of exercise and psychological variables including well-being, social support, stress and anxiety.

Of particular note in the survey was that people who exercise regularly in their youth are more likely to continue or to resume exercise in later years. 25 per cent of those active when aged 14 to 19 years were very active now, compared with 2 per cent active now who were inactive at that earlier age. There was also a clear association between past participation in sport and physical recreation and the prevalence of heart disease, angina and breathlessness. Among those who had not taken part in regular sport and recreation in adult life, 21 per cent of men and 15 per cent of women over the age of 55 suffered from one of those chronic conditions, compared with only 14 per cent and 3 per cent respectively who had regularly participated in sport for over three quarters of their adult years.

The most well–publicised result of this survey showed that nearly one third of men and two thirds of women would find it difficult to sustain walking at a reasonable pace (about 3 mph up a 1 in 20 slope). This has to be balanced against the fact that 80 per cent of both men and women of all ages believed themselves to be fit and the majority incorrectly believed that they did enough exercise to keep fit.

The reason for quoting from this survey is to show how important sport and recreation is not only to those who have an interest in participating, but to those who believe that they have no interest in sport at all. Everyone must take an interest in exercise if they wish to remain fit for life. The significance of this report has not been lost on the National Health Service or on the Health Education Authority and 'The Health of the Nation' campaign has been influenced by its findings.

So what significance does this have for a book about developing partnerships? One answer lies in the development of General Practitioner (GP) Referral schemes in the UK and their potential for increasing the revenue earning potential of local authority–owned sport and leisure centres. This is not about a partnership between the public and private sectors, but about a partnership between the public and public sectors — between local authorities and the NHS.

GP referral schemes

There are probably over 100 GP referral schemes running throughout the UK and if a local authority does not have one, then it is probably thinking of developing one. One of the first projects to be set up in this country was the Oasis Project at Hailsham which began in 1990. The Manager of the Lagoon Leisure Centre and initiator of the Oasis Project is Mike Osbourne and he has become an expert in this subject and regularly runs courses for local authorities, GPs or other NHS personnel who are interesting in setting up similar schemes.

Hailsham is a small town outside Lewes in East Sussex, which falls within Wealden District Council. Despite being situated in the South East of England, it is an area which has a high social depravation and where only 20 per cent of the population would be considered affluent.

Three years ago, Mike Osbourne and his fitness consultant Jim McLauchlan carried out research into the usage of The Lagoon, which was a traditional sports centre with a swimming pool, sports hall and health suite. They discovered that nothing would persuade 76 per cent of their population to use the sports centre, no matter what promotions were carried out or even if the cost of using the centre was reduced. They therefore realised that their marketing efforts were only reaching the converted and that how and when these people used the centre was dependent on the services provided and how they were treated.

Part of the problem arises from what Mike Osbourne calls the 'Chipbuttyman' — the overweight, unfit Mr or Mrs Average, who looks at the leisure centre as something only to be used by those who are fit. The Jane Fonda-like aerobics instructor puts them off and peer pressure makes them feel exposed.

These social and psychological clues to the usage of the average leisure centre were balanced in Hailsham by a Conservative led Council, who insisted that the leisure centre must break even and would not be given any revenue subsidy. Combined, these factors led to some soul searching about how usage of the centre could be increased. Increased usage would mean increased revenue.

The GP referral scheme started with a dozen patients referred by one GP. Forty GPs now take part in the project and since each of these general practitioners is probably seeing 300 patients per week, the potential supply of new users of the Oasis centre is enormous.

Most GPs have a number of what they would call 'heart sink' patients — that is those patients whose appearance at the surgery makes the doctor's heart sink! Up until now the only prescription available to doctors was some sort of tablet, consultant referral or consultation. The GP referral scheme offers an alternative answer for some of these patients through a prescription of exercise. The doctor decides what level of exercises is appropriate and therefore what exercise is prescribed at the leisure centre remains under their control.

Recent research at Hailsham has shown that of 36 per cent of people who were self-referred — i.e. they decided that they really must get fit after Christmas etc., continued to use the centre at the end of one year. For those patients referred by a GP, continuation on the programme is twice as high. It seems that if the doctor refers you, then it must be good for you and you will stick on the course.

In Hailsham, ten week courses were prescribed by the GP. At the end of that time, the patient is referred back to the GP and offered two months free use of the leisure centre. Since over 60 per cent of patients remain using the centre after one year, it follows that The Lagoon saw an increase in use of their facilities of over 15 per cent, when in most other districts in the area use of sports facilities was declining by 9 per cent.

Patients who could afford to pay something are asked to do so — £1.30 for fitness and 75p for a swim. If the doctor says that the patient cannot afford to make a contribution, then they do not pay.

In financial terms the average GP referral scheme will cost £5,000 to set up and for the length of the course, the increased revenue is nil. This is because the increased cost of staff required to cover the scheme is equal to the increased revenue. The potential profit for the centre comes, however, in the period after the course has ended and from the 60 per cent of 'referred patients' who continue to use the centre. In Hailsham, they believe that they have increased their revenue by £50,000 per annum — a significant sum for any local authority owned sports and leisure centre.

There are a number of significant political points to be made by GP referral schemes. On a local level, GP referral has transformed the Lagoon Leisure Centre from one that provides sporting activities to those who could afford it to one which addresses the needs of a much wider community. It has also made leisure the flagship of the local authority's perceived delivery of services to the local community.

Nationally, GP referrals have demonstrated that they have unique marketing tool which can significantly increase income for local authority leisure services. It also has the potential to make major savings for the National Health Service. Some preliminary research conducted in Hailsham indicated that the savings for each GP may be in the order of £150,000 per annum.

The greatest problem for Mike Osbourne and his staff is that so far they have failed to persuade their local Family Health Services Authority (FHSA) to contribute financially towards the programme. Therefore, their revenue savings have come purely from increased use of the centre.

The Oasis project has been extended from GP referrals to Community Services and Social Services. Staff from Community Services bring their patients into the centre so that they can share in the social benefits of coming together in an atmosphere where 'relaxation' is as important as exercise. Problems with isolation of post natal groups and day care centre groups has been greatly reduced. The success of the Community Health scheme prompted a new relationship with the Social Services. A short pilot study led to the setting up of Family Evenings - targeted specifically at family groups. In this instance the Social Services do pay for their clients to use the centre as a method of improving family bonding.

Research into the cost benefit of the Oasis Project is currently being undertaken by Brighton University. This research will analyse the cost benefit to the NHS, the leisure centre and central government. It is funded by the Primary Care Development Fund. More locally, the SE region of the Sports Council is funding research into using the Oasis programme as an alternative method of inducing minority groups to use leisure centres.

The next step for The Oasis project is to increase the number of more critical medical cases referred to the centre. Work with diabetics, who can use exercise as a means of balancing their insulin intake has enormous potential. There is potential for working with the geriatric unit of the local hospital, for working with the Coronary Care Clinic and the Orthopaedic Unit.

GP referral schemes elsewhere

Stockport, Preston, Southwark - these are just a few of the local authorities who have successful GP referral schemes. In Tyne and Wear a scheme called 'Wear Fit' extended the concept of GP referral through a mobile community based fitness team which worked in schools, local estates and with local companies. In the London Borough of Sutton, the District Health Authority is likely to fund a Co-ordinator Post for the project. In the Three Rivers District (between Watford and Hertford), the local health authority provided funding of £45,000 towards developing a fitness suite and the funding of a nurse to staff the facility. The scheme is aimed at the rehabilitation of coronary patients. In Hull, East Riding Health Authority have awarded the City Council a contract to introduce a leadership training project for playground games in primary schools. Problems of bullying can be reduced by supervised play — the project will be introduced into five schools.

There is obviously enormous potential for future partnership between local authority sport and leisure centres and the National Health Service. At present the benefits of the scheme appear to be more obvious to those who operate sport and leisure facilities rather than to the health service as a whole — although the long term benefits and emphasis on primary health care has to make it attractive to the NHS. Research commissioned by the Health Education Authority from the School of Education at Exeter University will be completed and hopefully published this year. The Exeter research has looked at eleven GP Referral schemes. In tandem, Keele University has undertaken a second study which has looked at Healthy Alliances. Again the results of this research should be published this year.

A working party, the Physical Activity Task Force, has been set up by the Department of Health and DNH between the Sports Council and the Health Education Authority, with representation from the Association of District Councils and Association of Metropolitan Councils to consider the potential for establishing Physical Activity Targets. With the emphasis on the Private Sector Finance Initiative (see page 6) there will be many opportunities in the future for local authorities to win contracts from health promotion boards to implement community projects involving a healthy lifestyle. This presents a real challenge for sport and recreation departments and represents an opportunity for attracting revenue funding in the future.

Sports development

The experience at Hailsham confirms that not only is the provision of physical facilities for sport and leisure important, but people have to be encouraged to use them. The 'Sport and Active Recreation Provision in Inner Cities' [6] which was sponsored by Business In Sport when it was produced in 1989 by Colin Moynihan, stated that facilities in inner cities needed to be "closer to and more in keeping with the community's needs".

Hull City Council has been at the forefront of pioneering work in the area of Sport Development and in 1989 set up the Hull Action Sport Project [7], which was to become the cornerstone of the City Council's sports development work. The project was jointly funded by the Sports Council (Yorkshire and Humberside) and the City Council. Hull was also an Urban Programme area and attracted funding of £260,000 from the programme for sport development. Now that this funding is at the end of its life, its success has led to funding being continued from another main stream programme.

The first priority for the Action Sport Project was to address the problem of low participation of inner city communities in sport and recreation. The programme also involved schemes for training of sports leaders, créche workers, awareness of opportunities and facilities, employment, advice, support for clubs and groups, some of which had not previously existed and the setting up of networks.

The Project worked in close co-operation with the Bransholme Community Forum, which established a partnership network of some thirty five service providers and agencies, both statutory and voluntary, who were working in the community. Hull is established as a World Health Organisation 'Healthy City' [8] and funds were made available for promoting work in this area via the Hull Action Sport. Funds were also made available from the Safer Cities Project[9], who put up £2,100 for a Women's Self Defence and Personal Awareness Course. In the first three years, the Partnership Network generated an additional £12,500 of financial support to enhance the Hull Action Sport Programme.

The project took full account of the Health of the Nation programme and the national message was reinforced locally by the Hull and Holderness Health and Lifestyle survey.

Partnership was the key theme for the City Council and in due course led to the setting up of the UK's first voluntary Housing Action Trust (HAT) in partnership with Central Government and the community. The North Hull HAT covers an area of 6,000 people with 2,109 dwellings — 2,108 were built pre-war. Unemployment in the HAT area was around 20 per cent. 30 per cent of the population was aged over 60, a quarter of the homes were single households and three quarters in receipt of housing benefit.

As part of the programme for the HAT, Hull City Council's Leisure Services Department set up a lifestyle project to build upon its experience of sports development. Lifestyle promoted a general awareness of the benefits of a healthy lifestyle, provided learning and training opportunities, developed a programme to ensure that a comprehensive range of sporting and associated opportunities were available. The Sports Council's regional office funded a partnership and resourcing officer and a sports development officer and the HAT board agreed a support budget of £83,000. What was interesting was that residents of the HAT area did not want 'a bright shiny leisure centre', but wanted an Action Sport type of team on the ground, working with them and for them.

Over four years, creative partnerships have given Hull additional revenue resources of £480,000 to fund the Sports Development Initiatives alone. This is a scheme which has received considerable national recognition, but sport development work is still in its infancy. It is obviously something that has much to offer, both for inner cities and rural communities and should be used to enhance the appeal of sport and leisure in all local authorities.

The Bolton initiative [10]

Quite apart from the part to be played by sport in health and law and order issues, its role in community development also includes training. In Bolton, Bolton Metro Leisure Services initiated a scheme to create a training centre of excellence in Bolton for leisure, tourism, retail and catering. The initiative focused on the development of leisure and tourism in Bolton as a way of creating jobs, working with employers in the Borough to ascertain their training needs. They sought to broaden and diversify the local economic base by encouraging new forms of employment, responding to the needs of local residents, developing vocational training programmes and making Bolton attractive to potential investors, visitors, local businesses and communities.

Current projects include funding from the North West Arts Board towards a training initiative within Arts. The Leisure Management DSO had an unstructured programme of training and development for their managers. The programme will aim to give managers a feeling of ownership of their own development programme and will include implementation of NVQs. The initiative will undertake research on the leisure, tourism and catering industries in the Bolton area and link with regional and national organisations.

Many private sector commercial leisure operators have difficulty in convincing local authorities that leisure offers opportunities for real jobs. Leisure is often seen as providing low paid, unskilled, part time work. In fact most major operators have very detailed training programmes and many have become accredited as offering National Vocational Qualifications. As an example, a nightclub will offer 60-75 jobs, 39 of them full-time. A licensed restaurant offers 25-50 jobs and ten-pin bowling, 45 jobs.

It is important that as part of any campaign to raise the profile of the sport and leisure industry that its significance as an employer is not underestimated. Partnerships between the public and private sectors of the type highlighted in Bolton are very important to this aim.

Notes and references

1. The Institute of Sports Sponsorship — 071 828 8771
2. The Croydon Sports Partnership — 081 760 5592
3. The Youth Charter for Sport — 0204 303550
4. The Duke of Edinburgh's Award, Charter for Business — 071 245 0991
5. The National Fitness Survey, available from The Sports Council. £50
6. *Sport and Active Recreation Provision in the Inner Cities — Report of the Minister for Sport's Review Group 1988/89*, published by the Department of the Environment.
7. Hull Sports Development — Ben Corr, Senior Recreation Officer, Hull City Council Recreation Department — 0482 223111
8. *Healthy Cities*, sponsored by the World Health Organisation, but no direct funding is available. For further information about this and other health related projects, contact UK Health for All Network, Appeal Box 101 Liverpool L69 5BE — 051 231 1009
9. The Safer Cities Programme was introduced by the Home Office in 1988. Initially 20 projects around the country had funding. All but four projects will close on 31 Mar 94 and 40 new projects will be set up with smaller grant aid available. Responsibility for this scheme will pass from the Home Office to DoE and the Single Regeneration Budget which will be administered by ten new regional offices. Contracts to administer the first ten new areas where Safer Cities Grants will be available have been won by Crime Concern and NACRO
10. The Bolton Initiative — 0204 28851

9

Potential problems and how to overcome them

The case studies examined in the previous chapter have been factual and there has been little analysis of what problems can arise, why they arise and how to overcome them. It would be invidious to comment on individual schemes without giving the partners themselves space to comment on their own position and the reasons why they felt the project did not succeed. However, it is hoped that individual local authorities and private sector companies will understand if some general comments are made about schemes where the partnership failed. Only by some sort of analysis of these trends can we understand how to make future partnership work more smoothly. There may be dozens of equally exasperating examples which are not featured here, but if a particular project is mentioned, it because it is worth making some a general point about the feasibility of that project.

Pressures within a local authority

We began by looking at the use of capital receipts and planning gain as a means of attracting private sector investment. If the developer is creating a scheme where no sport and leisure facilities are to be included, then the leisure department of the local authority may find it difficult to ensure that some slice of the capital receipt or planning gain reaches sport and leisure. The development department (may come under planning in another local authority) will probably argue that the local authority has a potential capital programme of something in the region of £80 million and that at the bottom of that list is any spending on sport or leisure facilities! Some local authorities may insist that the local authority does not link potential development sites for sale with specific schemes which require capital investment. Then if the scheme falls through, the local authority does not find that it has made a commitment to a particular project, which it must fund from another source to maintain its credibility with the local community. There is a much greater understanding today of the wider definition of sport and leisure and its importance to the everyday life of the community. If the leisure department is having difficulty in making itself heard, then identifying the role of sport in improving health through GP referral schemes or other health related projects or using sport as an activity to occupy people who might otherwise turn to crime is important. (see Chapter 7). We should not be naive and expect sport to solve all our problems, but its profile in a local authority should be higher than it is at present. Only if sport can be seen in a wider context will it be appreciated, particularly with the advent of unitary authorities.

Delays that lead to a partnership failure — the importance of competition

When we looked at some of the schemes that failed, it became clear that in some instances the inclusion of leisure as part of a development or requiring a planning gain can cause unacceptable delays for the private sector, which at the end of the day mean that the proposal falls apart (see the examples from Glasgow and Coventry on pages 55–56). The private sector often has difficulty in understanding why it takes a local authority so long to make decisions. Local authorities will argue that this is part of the democratic life of a local community —

possibly it is! An alternative view is that procrastination means that at the end of the day the local community will be the losers. Try not to set up a deal so complicated that by the time all the relevant parties have reached agreement, everyone has lost interest! However attractive a location is, it will not work if there is too much competition in a neighbouring area. The scheme in Coventry (page 56) which required the replacement of a bus station before the work on the commercial leisure could commence eventually fell apart. It was a very complicated proposal between a developer, operators and the bus station operator and obviously it took time to obtain agreement from all parties. Unfortunately, by the time agreement had been reached, planning permission had been granted for a commercial leisure scheme in the neighbouring authority of Rugby. Although this came under the control of another local authority, in reality this competing scheme developed within five minutes travelling time of the centre of Coventry. Commercial leisure is very dependent on catchment and however attractive a particular site may be, leisure cannot be developed there if there are existing facilities which are already taking customers. In another instance in Derby, there was a proposal for the redevelopment of a site for a new head office for Thorntons. Adjacent would have been cinema, bingo and a nightclub. Whilst negotiations were continuing, a different cinema operator applied for planning permission for a multiplex cinema on another site in the town. Despite the fact that the local authority was keen to encourage the mixed-use development, it decided that commercial logic would dictate how the two competing schemes could succeed. Inevitably, the more complicated mixed-use scheme took longer to agree and by this time, the cinema on another site had opened. The Thorntons site is still empty.

The provision of sporting facilities by the private sector

In chapter 6, we looked at potential partnership schemes in Croydon, Dartford and Chingford, where the local authority was looking to the private sector to provide what were essentially sports facilities. The private sector was expected to provide the capital for the scheme and run the facility without revenue subsidy. There are only particular circumstances where this will work.

Croydon Borough Council believed that their site for the Croydon Water Palace (page 57) was so well located that it could support the provision by the private sector of a leisure pool without any capital or revenue contribution to making it happen. Even in the heady days of development in the late 1980s, they could not find a developer who was prepared to put up the capital costs without some sort of planning gain elsewhere in the area. In other words, developers said let us have a site for offices in the town centre of Croydon and we will build you a leisure pool, but we will not put up the capital cost without this incentive.

In the case of Dartford Borough Council and Waltham Forest (Fantaseas — page 58), they found themselves approached by a developer who offered to put up the capital for the development of a leisure world and asked the local authority for nothing more than perhaps a guarantee of the sums concerned. Whether the guarantee was in place or not, is immaterial. However, it is more pertinent to discuss why both these schemes failed.

The Rank Organisation took quite a large proportion of the space available in Stoke, including a requirement to operate a leisure pool and dry ski slope. Quite apart from the experience that Rank has of operating leisure pools as owners of Butlins Holiday Worlds, it was also able to build the leisure pool because it was being offered sites for more commercial leisure facilities. This is more difficult to achieve if a developer is looking to tie up a series of independent operators, one of which must run a leisure pool or leisure ice, as a stand–alone facility. In the late 1980s there was a belief that if you made ice or water commercial enough, then it would make an operating profit and pay back its capital. With a history in the UK of inherent low entrance charges and the cost of maintaining ice or water based facilities, there has to be a very special formula to make this work. Realistically, if a local authority is going to insist on this type of facility as part of a private sector sport or leisure development, then it must be prepared to assist with capital funding, or be sure that this can be raised from a capital receipt available from other facilities on the site. A potential solution is the one that is being proposed in Barnet (Chapter 6, page 46). The developer, THI, is responsible for finding operators for the commercial leisure and for using the capital receipt raised to pay for the swimming pool.

Linked to the problem of capital funding is revenue contributions. At Milton Keynes (chapter 6, page 56), the Development Corporation gave First Leisure some 'in kind' assistance with the capital when asking them to provide and run an ice rink. Unfortunately the long-term costs of operating the ice rink eventually led to its closure. Few private sector owner-operators can live with a facility that will always lose money. Rank make it work through a deal whereby part of the capital cost is defrayed by cheap land or some sort of capital contribution to the non-commercial sports facilities. The problem for First Leisure was that the density of commercial leisure in Milton Keynes did not provide enough revenue cross-subsidy to cover the losses of the ice rink. In Dartford and Chingford (page 58) the operator had a facility that not only had to pay back its capital but also make an operating surplus. It is interesting that the same operator has built and is operating a leisure pool for Tyne and Wear Development Corporation (page 37). However, the Development Corporation has made a considerable capital contribution towards the building of the pool.

If we look towards the future, then it is quite possible that a private sector operator may run a swimming pool, ice rink or sports hall without revenue subsidy, particularly if the design and mix of facilities is right. They are, however, unlikely to contribute all the capital costs and run the facility without any involvement from the local authority. If in twenty years time the public is prepared to pay as much for a swim as it does for a trip to the cinema, that may change. (Alternatively, we may have developed a system whereby the disadvantaged are subsidised and everyone else pays a more realistic charge.) While we have a continuing policy of low entrance charges for using competing local authority-run facilities, the private sector will find it difficult and unattractive to provide and run a sports facility without any assistance.

Private sector management

There seems little reason why a leisure pool on such a valuable site in Croydon (page 57) should not have been run by the private sector at no cost to the local authority. Croydon are after all now running the Water Palace at an operational break-even. The problem more probably lay in Sunley's inexperience in the area of operational management. Several companies entered the world of CCT, or voluntary arrangement before CCT was introduced, and had their fingers burnt because they did not have the expertise to deliver. There has been a steep learning curve for all CCT operators and the ones that have succeeded best are those who either were run by people who came from a local authority background, or had experience or running other public sector management contracts, or had the experience of operating something which was closely related to sport, such as a tennis club or health club. A background as a contractor for either Sunley or for Rush & Tompkins was not really good enough to make Croydon or the Plaza (page 58) in Exeter work. It is, however, very easy to be critical of the private sector when their failure is often given such a public airing. When private sector companies are in trouble, their shareholders and the newspapers quickly come to hear of it. There needs to be an end to the 'them and us' way of thinking and more sharing of problem between public and private sector organisations who run local authority management contracts. As already noted in the chapter about CCT, there is no doubt that some DSO contractors are having difficulties in fulfilling the terms of the bid they made to their own local authority. Their learning curve is unlikely to be any less steep than the one of the first private sector companies who believed that they could make a good business out of running CCT contracts.

Design and build contracts

Some question marks have to be raised over the question of design and build in leisure projects. Several readers will be able to give very good examples of where a design and build project has worked well and proved to be cheaper. It has however to be recognised that design and build is a method of construction which has grown up out of a need to reduce costs when often individual design elements are repeats of a scheme built somewhere else the previous week. The design element can be simple or complicated, but it is an element of a building or indeed the whole structure that has been used before. This is rarely the case when designing leisure buildings and in particular when designing swimming pools or leisure pools. Swimming pools are immensely complicated buildings which often require a unique design and often that design needs monitoring when it is put in place on site. Design and build for leisure buildings can work, but the client, and in most cases this means the local authority, has to know what it is doing in controlling the project. Otherwise, cost overruns or design failures which can go on years after the project is completed will occur. In the 1990s, the use of project managers is becoming more and more common. Whether it is through a consultant architect, or a project manager, their use may be contribute much to the success or otherwise of the scheme.

10

The benefits of charitable status

Charitable trust status has considerable appeal for non-commercial sport and leisure centres. One of its greatest advantages is that sports centres run as charitable trusts are exempt 80 per cent of the Uniform Business Rate (UBR), which can reduce the deficit funding required by a local authority by a considerable sum. In Greenwich, where a kind of Worker's Co-operative has been set up to run all leisure facilities, it is estimated that the savings on UBR have reduced their costs by £400,000 per annum. When the Metropolitan Authority required the leisure department to reduce their costs, setting up this co-operative to run their sport and leisure facilities was seen as the only alternative to closing centres. Certain local authorities own trusts that were set up in the 1960s, like the Welwyn and Hatfield Trust for the Gosling Sports Stadium. These charitable trusts do not cause a problem, but there have been disagreements with the Audit Commission when local authorities seek to set up new trusts for sports facilities. Although it is acknowledged that local authorities have the power to set up charitable trusts for theatres and the arts, the Audit Commission believe that they do not have the power to set up charitable trusts for sport and recreation.

The solicitor to the Audit Commission, Tony Child, has made his thoughts on this issue well known. In addressing this subject, Mr Child distinguishes between two situations for local authorities. The first is where a local authority employs a contractor to manage or run facilities on behalf of the local authority. The authority continues to be the provider of those facilities and simply has someone to manage the facilities, whether that comes under CCT or otherwise. The second situation is where a company, or some other body, actually assumes responsibility for the provision of the service. Most of the issues concerned with the setting up of trusts are connected to the latter situation.

In Tony Child's view, local authorities have power under Section 145 of the Local Government Act 1972 to establish a company or trust for entertainment. In essence this section says that *"A local authority may do, or arrange for the doing of, or contribute to the expenses of the doing of, anything necessary or expedient for any of the purposes set out in that section, namely the provision of entertainment"*. This section includes, for example, facilities for dancing. It appears that this section was devised by the Department of Environment. Unfortunately, the corresponding section of the Local Authorities' (Miscellaneous Provisions) Act 1976, section 19, was drafted by the Department of Education. This section deals with powers for local authorities dealing with recreation, but unfortunately since there was no co-ordination with DoE, this section is not as wide in its definition as Section 145. It is the view of the Audit Commission that section 111 does not go far enough.

There has been some argument about whether a different section of the Local Government Act 1972 (section 111) establishes powers for a local authority to set up a company or trust, or that Part V of the Local Government and Housing Act 1989 gives recognition to the fact that section 111 of the 172 Act provides power to establish a company. Unfortunately, it is the view of the Audit Commission that neither section refers directly to powers for recreation or sport.

These views raise a number of issues which question the role of the local authority as a provider. Is it right that a local authority should set up a company and thereby pass over control to that company? Will the public interest be subordinated to private gain? Parliament has laid down services and powers for local authorities. Is it right that the local authority should pass on these powers to a third party? Looking at this from the perspective of the Audit Commission, if a local authority sets up a company then the activities of that company fall at a stroke outside the remit of the district auditor. A certain degree of public accountability is lost. There is no doubt that setting up a charitable trust for sport and leisure facilities previously managed by the authority does take these facilities outside the direct control of a local authority.

Well, we cannot have it both ways. To begin with, the provision of sport and leisure facilities is not a statutory provision — it is only discretionary. As much of this book has indicated, Central Government is bound to a course which will encourage private sector investment in many schemes and institutions that were previously the sole preserve of the public sector. It is very difficult to see why a private sector company should invest in these facilities if total control remains with the local authority or any other public sector body. If local authorities are to be seen in future as enablers, then some part of their total control over the services they offer will inevitably be lost. It is inevitable that the setting up of a trust will reduce costs and it also offers a greater opportunity to encourage private sector investment.

There are literally hundreds of charitable trusts that exist, set up by local authorities for entertainment and the arts. There are many other trusts like the Gosling Sports Stadium Trust which were set up prior to any questioning of the trust system for sport. Most of these trusts work well and the local authorities who own them can point to the savings they make. There is no reason why a trust for sport should not be set up by a third party and there is every reason why trusts should be used in public/private sector partnership schemes.

In 1992, Business In Sport and Leisure [1] wrote a paper, which in due course was submitted through the Department of National Heritage to the Audit Commission and the Charity Commissioners for comment. The paper examined the role of charitable trusts in partnership schemes.

The paper considers how charitable status can be obtained. To obtain charitable status, it is necessary to persuade the Charity Commissioners that the provision of sport and leisure facilities are run on a charitable basis. The history of cases brought before the Charity Commission date from 1895. In general, charitable status has only been allowed for organisations providing sport and recreation facilities under two headings. The first qualification is where an organisation is providing physical education for youngsters, i.e. at school and university. The alternative is where the facilities qualify as recreation facilities under the Recreational Charities' Act 1958, if they are for the public benefit and "in the interests of social welfare". The 'social welfare' test is satisfied if the facilities improve the conditions of life for users and either the users need the facilities because of their youth, age, infirmity, disablement, poverty or social and economic circumstances or the facilities are available to the public at large. In recent years, the Charity Commissioners have been happy to accept sports facilities for charitable status, so long as the facilities will be open for everyone to use. This means that the centre cannot be operated on a membership basis, or in some way be restrictive. Centres of excellence can have problems with charitable status if they are used for training elite performers — in other words not everyone can use them all of the time. The only other problem for the Charity Commissioners is that the centre is non-profit making and that any profit it does make will go back into the charity —it cannot be distributed to shareholders. Applications for charitable status need to be careful that their brochures are not too full of the bar and café facilities operated by the centre — these activities are not charitable!

In 1993, at the instigation of the Department of National Heritage, the Sports Council in conjunction with the National Playing Fields Association and the Central Council of Physical Recreation (CCPR), published a brochure on 'Sport and Charitable Status' [2]. The brochure is based upon material prepared by Richard Baldwin of Touche Ross & Co. The brochure outlines the benefits of charitable status and seeks to encourage sports clubs and voluntary bodies to apply for charitable status.

The BISL paper considers that many commercial leisure owner-operators are keen to enter into partnerships with local authorities in return for planning gain. A number of examples we looked at in chapter 6 concern the building of non-profit making swimming pools, ice rinks or sports halls in return for planning permission for commercial leisure, i.e. cinema, ten-pin bowling, nightclubs, hotels and pubs. One of the key problems of such partnerships, particularly when providing community sports facilities, is keeping entrance charges low. This should ensure that the facility is open to every section of the community to use, whatever their means. The answer may be through the setting up by the private sector company of a charitable trust for the non-profit making part of the scheme.

To use a hypothetical example: a local authority needs a new swimming pool, but has a site that is attractive to the private sector and will take ten-pin bowling, a restaurant and a nightclub. There are few problems for the private sector in raising the capital to build the swimming pool, but in the long term the operating deficit of possibly £50,000-£250,000 is unacceptable. However, the private sector could buy the land and offer a long lease to a charitable trust set up to run the swimming pool. (The private sector would therefore retain its long term land holding.) The trustees would be made up of members of the private sector company, the local authority and local business and sports representatives. The trust would be exempt from at least 80 per cent of UBR and the swimming pool could still be subsidised by the local authority to allow local people of all financial means to be able to use it. The swimming pool would therefore be a true community facility.

In due course the paper written by BISL was approved by the Charity Commission and by the Audit Commission. On Wednesday 9th June 1993, Hansard published the House of Lords' Sports Debate. In this, the Viscount Astor, Government spokesman on National Heritage, referred to the BISL paper:

"An important theme of the Government's approach to the provision of sports facilities is that we would move away from the concepts of separate local authority sports facilities and separate private sector commercial leisure. The Government are keen to encourage partnerships and many have already been created successfully. Charitable trusts can also be used to assist such partnerships and keep entrance fees low. That has been suggested by the commercial leisure operators represented by Business In Sport and Leisure in its discussions with the Association of District Councils and others."

BISL is continuing to work on the notion of using charitable trusts to encourage partnerships for sport and leisure facilities and is working with Touche Ross and Jacques and Lewis (solicitors) to expound on these views[3].

Notes and references

1. BISL paper on charitable trusts, available from BISL

2. *Sport and Charitable Status*, published by the Sports Council

3. Jaques & Lewis — contact Rod Ainsworth or John Glasson — 071 919 4500; Touche Ross — contact Richard Baldwin — 071 936 3000

Guidelines on how to set up and develop partnerships

Much of what has been written in preceding chapters highlights the benefits of partnerships and opportunities for the future. But how are these partnerships set up, who approaches who and how can the partnership develop? In researching this subject and in talking to many private sector operators and their local authority partners, many of the following points have been raised.

For the local authority

The first question is who to approach and what homework must be done before you start. Most private sector operators are prepared to discuss an idea. A local authority may start with an idea that it wishes to attract private sector investment, but is unsure how to go about it. There are a number of avenues which can be explored. One answer is to approach a consultant who may be an architect, quantity surveyor, engineer or contractor. It may be that the local authority feels that the best route is through the preparation of a feasibility study and may therefore approach a consultancy company [1]. Another route is through a firm of surveyors who specialise in knowledge of which operators are interested in expanding which facilities and once the local authority has decided that it wishes to attract ten-pin bowling, cinema or bingo, then the surveyors will know who to ask and advice on the valuation of the site [2]. Organisations like BISL can be approached for a list of their members which combines names and addresses and details of what services companies offer or what facilities they operate [3].

Most owner-operators of commercial leisure are very happy to be approached direct. By using this method, local authorities will know from the start if their catchment is the right size and configuration to attract commercial leisure. If a site has not been chosen, the operator can be asked to give his views on where the leisure facilities should be located. Leisure is a very broad title — potential partners could be interested in operating anything from a pub to bingo, from a hotel to a nightclub, from ten-pin bowling to a cinema. (See page 23 for a more detailed list.) If the local authority decides that the site is so complicated, or requires a mixed-use approach, then it may be that they need to approach a developer. There are not that many developers who specialise in leisure development, but there are a few. Even if a developer is approached, or approaches the local authority, if commercial leisure is to be a strong component part of the scheme, then it is often worth checking the requirements of the individual operators. It can be very easy for a developer to promise whatever the local authority requires, for example that the cinema will show a series of films for ethnic minorities. The problem then comes when the developer ties up the deal with the operator who is totally unprepared to honour the terms and conditions offered to the local authority!

The importance of location of a site and of catchment cannot be stressed more strongly. The best site in the world right on a motorway or main road junction will not attract commercial leisure operators if the catchment is not considered sufficient. The document 'Planning for Commercial Leisure' (see page 24) gives broad guidelines on the catchment required for 19 different kinds of leisure facilities. Obviously these guidelines are only general and it should also be stressed that most of the operating companies who contributed to this document are fairly large companies. It may be that a local company will be interested in taking on the site and may not have such rigorous requirements for location or catchment. The only risk may be their ability to fund the operation and their track record. It is also quite possible that the potential premium or rent will also decrease.

Once the site has been identified, the local authority will probably decide to issue some sort of development brief. One of the problems for leisure operators who are interested in buying land from local authorities is that any approach cannot be considered in isolation. As an example, a major pub retailer approached a local authority with an idea for converting a historic building that had fallen into disrepair. The local authority was then forced to go out to the market and advertise or approach other pub retailers to see if they would offer a better price for the site. This requirement for a local authority is a very understandable legacy of 'Polson'. It does however dampen the enthusiasm of operators approaching a local authority to buy a site which they believe has some potential. One answer that has been suggested is that if an operator approaches a local authority and offers a price for a site, then the local authority could have the site valued by an independent surveyor. If the operator is offering a similar sum, then the site could be theirs without recourse to advertising the site to the operator's competitors.

If the development is a large one, then an advertisement to invite interested developers and operators to bid for it is obviously necessary. It is really very important for the private sector that the local authority has a comprehensive and well thought through development brief. So many partnership schemes fall apart, or take years to come to fruition because of a flaw in the initial brief. If the brief is issued by the development department, then it is vital that the planning department is happy with the level of development proposed. A leisure brief separate from a planning brief will not work (see example at Cambridge Parkside, page 34) and these departments must work together to ensure that they are in agreement before the private sector is invited to tender. Schemes can be delayed indefinitely if the site involves compulsory purchase or the landowner is not the local authority. The local authority may think that it owns the land and then discover that they have a long lease from the County Council, or Town Council, or that there is some sort of covenant on the land to prevent certain types of development or to preserve public open space.

The importance of a single point of contact cannot be overstated. It is enormously helpful for the private sector if one person in the local authority has overall responsibility for the scheme (see Bracknell, page 13, Hemel Hempstead, page 45, Guildford, page 33) Inevitably there will be delays and the democratic nature of a local authority demands that decisions are taken by various committees and political parties. A single point of contact with a local authority officer who is determined to see that the project actually comes to fruition in invaluable.

Decide what is and what is not negotiable before negotiations are entered into. There are certain powers held in trust by a local authority which they will never willingly relinquish. The political persuasion of the local authority may well influence decisions and it is wise to sort out any potential areas of conflict before the private sector is invited to discussions. The local authority may be totally against any form of membership club, or determined that their DSO will manage the completed building. It is as well to sort out these issues before you begin.

Once the project is up and running and you are down to a negotiation with one developer or one operator, make sure that the local authority has the right sort of professional advice. Many local authority do not have their own legal or architectural departments. It may be worth taking on independent advisors to ensure that you do not agree to something that you then regret. The private sector is not comprised entirely of sharks out to make a killing! They do however have to make a profit on any scheme and will do their best to negotiate a good deal for their company and shareholders.

The advice to take on independent advisors also applies to assessments of potential partners and their ability to fulfil the terms of the contract. Unless the local authority has great experience of a particular sector, it is always worth having an independent advisor who really does know this market. Several partnerships have fallen apart because the chosen private sector company does not have the financial resources to fulfil the contract. Leisure is very specialised and the market quite small. Decisions on the choice of partner should not always be made on their ability to promise the biggest and the best — they may not be able to fulfil this. If the partner is a developer, check independently that he really has the interest of commercial owner-operators of leisure and that these interested operators will build and manage the facility in the way you envisage.

For the private sector

Understanding a local authority is not easy. Cultural differences between a private sector company operating for profit and a local authority who are providing a service for the local community is not something that is easy to understand. A successful private sector company will probably be run by directors who are entrepreneurial, fast–moving and decisive. It is often difficult for these individuals to understand a local authority who may be indecisive, make decisions by committee and whose knowledge of modern leisure may be somewhat limited.

Patience is vital, as is an understanding of democratic accountability to a local community. Set realistic time frames for projects which do not overestimate the ability of the local authority to respond to requests. Even if the development brief if a good one, time taken to obtain planning, both outline and full, will be required. Realistic time frames are essential.

The cost of bidding for a site differs enormously, but when the owner is the local authority, it quite likely that various presentations will be required, particularly if you are entering a development competition. Some development briefs require the production of models, brochures and presentation plans. Do not underestimate the time needed to explain what you are trying to achieve. Even if the officer you are dealing with knows exactly what you are proposing, councillors come from all walks of life and their knowledge of modern leisure trends are likely to be limited. Modern nightclubs are very different from the discotheques of the past. Operators are looking at different markets — they may be looking to attract teenagers, or the over 25s. As the public's expectations of quality services from a local authority has risen, so have customer expectations of commercial leisure facilities. A much higher standard of interior design and comfort is essential. Some local authorities and local communities are categorically opposed to certain forms of commercial leisure such as amusements, nightclubs, multiplex cinema or bingo, without really understanding what the modern concept of these centres are all about. The recent move from amusements to family fun centres is a good example of the type of changes that are taking place. Much time may need to be devoted to explaining modern concepts — it is unlikely to be time wasted.

There has already been some mention of the need of the local authorities to invite tenders to achieve the best price. If the site you are looking for is owned by a local authority then this is probably absolutely necessary.

Do not be arrogant. One local authority described the presence of a employee from a private sector leisure company as a "second hand car salesman"! Most local authorities, whatever their political persuasion, are very conventional. You are expected to appear before a meeting of the full council in a jacket and tie. Perhaps this is another way of saying that approach, modes of address and appearance are as important as the quality of the scheme you are proposing! Local authorities are looking for partners that they can trust and if you conform to their expectations of a respectable partner, you are more likely to be chosen.

Some time must be taken in assessing who holds the balance of power. Some local authorities are dominated by their officers, others by their councillors. Much heartache can be avoided if you take the time to discover if the person you are dealing with is likely to make the final decision about the go-ahead for your scheme.

Above all, be aware that you are dealing with a publicly–funded body who are guardians of the public purse and accountable to local people.

Notes and references

1. Leisure Consultants who may be approached include KPMG Peat Marwick, Touche Ross, Horwath and Strategic Leisure.

2. Surveyors who specialise in leisure and who may be approached include Humberts Leisure, Edward Symmons and Partners and Hearn and Partners.

3. List of Members of BISL available from 7 Soho Street, London W1V 5FA.

12

Conclusion

Much of what has been written so far extols the benefits of partnerships as a way forward for the future. To summarise these benefits, it is worth thinking about the following points:

- For whatever reason, local authorities are reducing the funds available to pay for the sporting and leisure aspirations of their community. It makes much sense to look towards the private sector for assistance with capital or revenue funding.

- The private sector is much more interested than people think in entering into partnerships with local authorities and there are plenty of examples of good practice contained in this book.

- Most partnerships for capital funding raise investment which would be beyond the reach of many local authorities. Whatever the priorities within the local authority for the provision of other services, the provision of sport and leisure facilities is vital to the well–being of your community. The campaign for 'The Health of the Nation' for fitter, more active population, requires the provision of facilities where people can participate in physical activity. The correlation between providing facilities where people can relax, and take part in active and passive pursuits can and will reduce crime, especially in youngsters.

- Reducing revenue budgets for local authorities is as important as raising capital. Local authorities should not be caught by thoughts that the private sector can manage their facilities better than they do at present. That may or may not be so. What is more important is that the private sector probably has the ability to make other types of investments in the facilities that they manage which would be beyond the scope of local authority.

- Partnerships can be with major public companies and large operators or developers, or with locally–based private businesses and small operators. They can cover capital investment, revenue investment, sponsorship, sports development and local cooperation.

- It has only been possible in this book to scratch the surface of examples of best practice. We have tried to consider partnership schemes in many different geographical locations:

    in inner cities
    in rural communities
    in tourist areas.

- Capital has been raised through planning gain, or capital receipt, through extended management contracts and through leasing.

- Revenue subsidy has been reduced through sponsorship, extended or varied CCT contracts, voluntary arrangements or leases.

So what of the future?

If local authorities are to be seen as true enablers, then partnership is a way forward for us all. It will only work if both the public and private partner really wants to make it work. There are many pitfalls, but far more examples of good practice which I hope this book has highlighted. The development of good sport and leisure facilities is something which we should all be working towards, not only to provide opportunities to develop our international athletes of the future, but also to encourage participation, an occupation and a healthy way of life. Partnership is one real answer which is worth exploring together.

Without a crystal ball, it is always difficult to assess trends. However, recent articles in both Leisure Week and Leisure Management have shown the increasing interest of private sector companies to invest in sport. Redelco, partners in Kettering (page 39) have announced a new scheme in partnership with Sefton Borough Council in Southport. Interhaus Sport, partners in the Norwich Sport Village (page 35) have announced a second scheme in Folkestone. The investment by First Leisure in ISL and the investment of Invicta Leisure in tennis, all point to a strengthening of interest in sport and the important part it plays in life. Some of the most imaginative schemes we have looked at in chapter 7, show how CCT contracts and voluntary arrangements can assist with capital and revenue investment in sport. In the future, it is hoped that some support will be made available from the National Health Service as interest grows in GP referral schemes and healthy alliances for Primary Health Care.

Private sector owner-operators of commercial leisure facilities have always been there, but as the UK emerges from recession there will be increased interest in acquiring sites from local authorities. Partnership is a term that must be given a wide interpretation. Funding from the National Lottery is a goal in the future that we must all aspire to, but this should be seen as another incentive to look for partners to take these new schemes forward as we approach the millennium.

Index